PUT YOUR
MONEY
WHERE YOUR
LIFE IS

D0167733

OTHER BOOKS BY MICHAEL H. SHUMAN

The Local Economy Solution (2015)

Local Dollars, Local Sense (2012)

The Small-Mart Revolution (2006)

Going Local (1998)

PUT YOUR MONEY WHERE YOUR LIFE IS

How to Invest Locally Using Self-Directed IRAs and Solo 401ks

MICHAEL H. SHUMAN

Bestselling author of *The Small-Mart Revolution*

FOREWORD BY MORGAN SIMON

Berrett–Koehler Publishers, Inc.

Copyright © 2020 by Michael Shuman

All rights reserved. No part of this publication may be reproduced, distributed, or transmitted in any form or by any means, including photocopying, recording, or other electronic or mechanical methods, without the prior written permission of the publisher, except in the case of brief quotations embodied in critical reviews and certain other noncommercial uses permitted by copyright law. For permission requests, write to the publisher, addressed "Attention: Permissions Coordinator," at the address below.

Berrett-Koehler Publishers, Inc.
1333 Broadway, Suite 1000
Oakland, CA 94612-1921
Tel: (510) 817-2277
Fax: (510) 817-2278
www.bkconnection.com

ORDERING INFORMATION

Quantity sales. Special discounts are available on quantity purchases by corporations, associations, and others. For details, contact the "Special Sales Department" at the Berrett-Koehler address above.

Individual sales. Berrett-Koehler publications are available through most bookstores. They can also be ordered directly from Berrett-Koehler: Tel: (800) 929-2929; Fax: (802) 864-7626; *www.bkconnection.com*.

Orders for college textbook / course adoption use. Please contact Berrett-Koehler: Tel: (800) 929-2929; Fax: (802) 864-7626.

Distributed to the U.S. trade and internationally by Penguin Random House Publisher Services.

Berrett-Koehler and the BK logo are registered trademarks of Berrett-Koehler Publishers, Inc.

Printed in the United States of America

Berrett-Koehler books are printed on long-lasting acid-free paper. When it is available, we choose paper that has been manufactured by environmentally responsible processes. These may include using trees grown in sustainable forests, incorporating recycled paper, minimizing chlorine in bleaching, or recycling the energy produced at the paper mill.

Library of Congress Cataloging-in-Publication Data
Names: Shuman, Michael, author.
Title: Put your money where your life is : how to invest locally through self-directed IRAs and solo 401ks / by Michael H. Shuman.
Description: First edition. | Oakland, CA : Berrett-Koehler Publishers, [2020] | Includes bibliographical references and index.
Identifiers: LCCN 2019054231 | ISBN 9781523088904 (paperback) | ISBN 9781523088911 (pdf) | ISBN 9781523088928 (epub)
Subjects: LCSH: Investments. | Self-directed individual retirement accounts. | 401(k) plans.
Classification: LCC HG4521 .S555 2020 | DDC 332.024/0145—dc23
LC record available at https://lccn.loc.gov/2019054231

First Edition
27 26 25 24 23 22 21 20   10 9 8 7 6 5 4 3 2 1

Book producer and text designer: Happenstance Type-O-Rama
Cover designer: Rob Johnson, Toprotype, Inc.

*To Cathy Berry, Guy Bazzani,
the late Dick Lahn, Roy Pollock,
and Kate Poole, all of whom
generously invested in me and
made this book possible*

Candide Group, LLC ("Candide Group") is a California state registered investment advisor located in Oakland, California. The content in the Foreword has been provided for informational purposes only and is not intended to serve as investment, tax, or legal advice or as a recommendation for the purchase or sale of any security. The information and opinions stated in the Foreword reflect Morgan Simon's views as of the time of publication and are subject to change.

The information and opinions contained within Put Your Money Where Your Life Is *reflect the views of Michael Shuman and not necessarily those of Morgan Simon or Candide Group. Any investment advice or financial planning advice contained herein have been offered solely by the author. Candide Group's specific advice is given only within the context of our contractual agreements with each client. Candide Group and Morgan Simon are not responsible for the consequences of any decisions or actions taken as a result of the information provided herein and do not guarantee the accuracy or completeness of the information provided in this book.*

CONTENTS

LIST OF CHARTS AND BOXES

Charts

Boxes

FOREWORD

Where Does Your Money Spend the Night?

The vast majority of us have no idea where our money spends the night. When we turn over our money to the bank, or to a financial advisor, or to a retirement plan, it can feel as though it's not ours anymore. And like anything that happens behind closed doors, this can make us nervous—will we achieve our financial goals? And for those of us who try to live ethically in other areas of our life—is our money being used to help or harm others?

The sad truth is that the economy has largely been designed to harm, not help. That's what led me to cofound Candide Group, a Registered Investment Advisor that helps families, foundations, athletes, and other cultural influencers who want their money working for social justice. Our company is named after the Voltaire novel, which talks about wrestling with the forces of good and evil—which is what we do every day as impact investors.

When we get money wrong, we wind up with fossil fuel companies and private prisons. When we get money right, we get renewable energy and more ownership and autonomy for grassroots communities. We start to repair historic harms and transform our society. And when we do it right, we are able to effectively plan for the future, a future where our individual families have built the wealth they need to thrive and can live in thriving communities with others. As Indigenous activists like Lilla Watson have taught us, because our liberation is bound together inextricably, building "wealth" by harming others will never be fulfilling.

How do we move our money from the old paradigm to this newer, happier place, an economy that effectively serves us? We start by knowing where it spends the night. We seek out community banks and credit unions that keep our money local. We hold financial advisors accountable for the impact of their decisions. We map our power—perhaps you are an alumna of a university with a billion dollar endowment, or a teacher or city worker who is part of a trillion dollar pension fund, and can encourage that endowment or fund to make more ethical decisions. And as Michael Shuman explains in this important book—you can take control of your own retirement savings.

In the pages that follow, you will learn about the ways you can shift your IRAs, 401ks, and 403bs into local businesses, projects, and people you care about. Some of Shuman's suggestions are deeply personal—getting ourselves or our kids out of credit card debit or paying off our mortgage, for instance. Others propose learning about new investment opportunities in our broader community—in food co-ops, bookstores, and community land trusts, for example—and then using what he calls "DIY Accounts" to move our tax-deferred savings into them. With these sorts of investments, you always know where your money spends the night.

I applaud you for pushing past some very reasonable fears in picking up this book. In my own work, I have helped move tens of millions into social investing every year and know just how difficult it can be to pick great investments. But in my journey from activist to investment advisor, I've learned that the financial services industry benefits from being intentionally opaque and making us all feel as if we can't do this ourselves. So many of the pioneers in impact investing started out precisely by pushing past that fear with a strong belief that we could do it better.

And guess what—from *Harvard Business Review* to BlackRock,[1] numerous traditional institutions have come out saying that companies that take the environment and communities into account do indeed perform better. Private prison companies have lost 30 percent of their stock value over the past year as the public pushes back against their human rights abuses.[2] As I write this, $11 trillion has been divested from fossil fuels, yet another dying industry.[3] Yet traditional advisors tend to stick to the usual adage: "No one gets fired for buying General Electric." In the last downturn, traditional investors lost trillions of dollars,[4] whereas impact investors, who by nature lean toward a focus on longer-term outcomes, tended to weather the storms better and have more stability as they move into retirement.[5] The potential for less volatility and more community benefit sounds like a win-win to me—and is part of why one in every four dollars from retail investors is now engaged in some sort of social investment.[6]

But even as impact investing has gone mainstream, a lot of it is indeed impact washing from traditional financial institutions who think you can know how to change the world by looking down from a fortieth-story Manhattan high-rise. As I note in my book, *Real Impact: The New Economics of*

Social Change, we have the opportunity to get impact investing wonderfully right or terribly wrong depending on how
much community accountability we can structure into our
processes.

In contrast, Shuman's approach is all about local community building and responding to deep community desires
and needs. It redefines the notion of expert—as we are all
the experts of our lived experiences and all of us can make
intelligent decisions about how to spread money in our communities. We just need some courage, conviction, and a
roadmap—which Shuman so gracefully provides.

MORGAN SIMON

Cofounder of Candide Group and author of *Real Impact:
The New Economics of Social Change*

PREFACE

Americans agree on very little these days. Yet there is one point on which red state conservatives and blue state progressives are increasingly united: Wall Street can no longer be trusted.

The near collapse of the global economy in 2008, caused in part by radioactive mortgage products sold and resold by thousands of once-beloved financial institutions, threw millions of Americans out of work, forced many to lose their homes, and stole trillions of dollars from their life savings. Unemployment has since dropped, the stock market has roared back, our pensions have largely recovered, but most of us cannot completely forget how close the economy came to total meltdown.

One sign of the lingering distrust is that the 2016 presidential race saw not one but two of the top candidates—Donald Trump and Bernie Sanders—campaign against Wall Street. Their messages, and the similar messages now heard from their 2020 rivals, resonated with tens of millions of Americans who remain nervous tethering their financial futures to so many unfamiliar, unreliable, and unethical financiers.

But what's the alternative? There isn't much of one, unfortunately. At least that's the common wisdom. Most of us continue to invest our money in the stocks and bonds of the world's biggest companies we barely understand. Our mutual fund managers, pension fund representatives, and investment advisors insist these investments are the best bets for growing our wealth.

Superficially, we are given many choices: Value or growth companies. Big cap or small cap. Stocks or bonds. US-based or foreign businesses. Socially responsible or not. But in the end, all these investment choices are more limited than we think.

There *are* real alternatives, but few of us consider them. You can invest in everything else that matters to you. You can put your money into that neighborhood grocery store you love, your little sister's first house, or your nephew who needs to pay off high-interest student loans. If you're smart about local investing, you can do this in a way that increases your financial returns compared to Wall Street and lowers your risk. Plus, these commonsense local investments wind up strengthening your community, your neighborhoods, and your schools.

If you're interested in how to get your tax-deferred savings out of global companies you distrust and into everything else you love, you've picked up the right book. In the pages ahead, you will learn how you can deploy two well-established—but rarely used—tools to expand your investment options. These are the Self-Directed IRA and the Solo 401k. This book aims to dispel all the myths, confusions, and worries about these do-it-yourself tools—and will show you how you can deploy them to improve both your and your community's bottom lines.

MICHAEL SHUMAN
Silver Spring, Maryland
February 2020

INTRODUCTION

Pop quiz! Please answer the following three questions:

- Have you mindfully bought local goods and services over the last week? For example, were you drawn to a farmers' market, a locally owned hardware store, or a local crafts fair?

- Do you have a checking or savings account at a locally owned bank, thrift, or credit union?

- If you have any savings for your retirement, have you invested at least 1 percent in your local businesses, your city's newest development projects, or your neighbors?

For the past twenty-five years, I've put these questions to more than a thousand audiences across North America—in all, probably several hundred thousand people. And the results are always the same.

- The vast majority care deeply about their local economies and have dramatically shifted their buying habits. They are flocking in expanding numbers to local brew pubs, farm-to-table restaurants, credit unions, cooperatives, and businesses proudly proclaiming themselves as "Locally Owned."

- Fewer than half bank locally. The Move Your Money campaign launched after the 2008 financial meltdown convinced more than a million people to shift their money from Wall Street banks to local banks and credit unions. But most Americans continue to conduct their daily financial transactions at a few increasingly powerful global banks like Citigroup, JPMorgan Chase, and Wells Fargo.

- On the last question about retirement funds, the answer is stunning. Typically one or two hands pop up, and—honestly—these folks turn out to be mistaken. Even though local businesses comprise 60–80 percent of our economy (depending on how we define "local"), and many are highly profitable and competitive, Americans don't think twice about placing more than 99 percent of their life savings in global businesses they don't know and often distrust.

We care deeply about the shops and people in our daily lives, but we do not know how to apply this intention to our own money. All of us, even the most resolute anti-globalization activists, systematically overinvest in Wall Street and underinvest in Main Street. We want to support our local businesspeople, our city's infrastructure, our neighbors, and our kids, and yet when it comes to our money, we happily surrender it to financiers hundreds or thousands of miles away.

Imagine pulling off the highway and finding the House of Broc, a diner that serves only broccoli. To be sure, many variations of broccoli are on the menu—broccoli salads, broccoli casseroles, broccoli shakes, broccoli ice cream—but you might feel inclined to point out the obvious. Where are the other vegetables like carrots, zucchini, and spinach? How about beef, chicken, and fish? This book is about pointing out how many delicious and healthful alternatives can and should be on the investment menu.

It's tempting to ascribe our habit of keeping our money as far away from our lives as possible to a sinister conspiracy involving greedy bankers, corrupt politicians, and gullible citizens. I won't. The real explanation is more interesting. It's a story of good intentions gone awry. We enacted securities laws in the 1930s designed to protect investors from fraudsters, but the perverse effect was to create a system of finance so complex that only the biggest players—big investors on one side, big business on the other—could afford to jump through the expensive legal hoops and play. Over time, innovations like mutual funds pried open this system for the rest of us, and today we participate in this system through workplace plans like 401ks and private Individual Retirement Accounts (IRAs). But the system still funnels money almost exclusively into large, publicly traded companies.

In recent years two revolutions have taken place in the world of finance, one well known and the other largely invisible. The first revolution concerns the mission of business and investment. The traditional view was well articulated by the noted conservative economist Milton Friedman, who wrote in 1970, "There is one and only one social responsibility of business—to use its resources and engage in activities designed to increase its profits."[1]

Almost half a century later, the Business Roundtable released a statement from 181 top CEOs redefining "corporate responsibility" as needing to incorporate not just shareholders but also stakeholders like workers, suppliers, the home community, and the environment. Jamie Dimon, chair of JPMorgan Chase and chair of the Roundtable, said, "The American dream is alive, but fraying. Major employers are investing in their workers and communities because they know it is the only way to be successful over the long term. These modernized principles reflect the business community's unwavering commitment to continue to push for an economy that serves all Americans."[2]

The Business Roundtable declaration is just the latest example of a revolutionary new view about business. In 1997, the author John Elkington coined the term "triple bottom line" to refer to the performance of a company not just in terms of its profitability but also its benefit to workers, suppliers, communities, and ecosystems.[3] Since then commentators sometimes refer to these bottom lines as the three Es (economy, equity, and ecology) or the three Ps (profit, people, and planet).

The concept of "corporate social responsibility" was initially defined in negative terms. The first socially responsible investment funds, like Calvert and Pax World, screened out investments in manufacturers of weapons or cigarettes, or firms doing business in apartheid South Africa. Over time, these screens became positive, so that "impact investors" could focus on companies that were delivering renewable energy, affordable housing, or pollution cleanup. One recent estimate is that about a quarter of all investment worldwide—$20 trillion—is being done through screens factoring in environmental, social, and governance (ESG) concerns.[4]

As investors have rethought their priorities, so have businesses seeking responsible investors' money. Companies like Ben & Jerry's, The Body Shop, and Stonyfield raised the bar on social responsibility, and dozens, then hundreds, of companies followed.[5] Today, more than three thousand companies have gone through a rigorous process to become "B Corps" (the "B" stands for beneficial), the best-known standard of high corporate good behavior, and tens of thousands of other companies regularly use the B metrics to improve their social performance.

"Impact investing," however, is largely about big investors putting their money into big companies. Which brings us to the second revolution that few know about and even fewer have acted on—the grassroots investment revolution. It's now considerably cheaper and easier for local businesses, cities with development projects, and even individuals to raise money from customers, residents, and neighbors. Perhaps the most important date marking this revolution was April 5, 2012. That's when President Obama signed a revolutionary law legalizing crowdfunding called the Jumpstart Our Business Startups (JOBS) Act.

The term "crowdfunding" refers to many people each putting small amounts of money into an exciting business or project. (See adjacent box.) Before the JOBS Act, crowdfunding was mostly about making donations on websites like Kickstarter or interest-free loans through nonprofits like Kiva. You could get a perk like a T-shirt or a product sample, but actually making money—what most investors seek to accomplish—was forbidden.

Four Flavors of Crowdfunding

The term "crowdfunding" refers to at least four different flavors of local investment, all of which allow many people to put small amounts of money into businesses. The first flavor, donation crowdfunding, is arguably not an investment at all, since you get only a community rate of return, not a private one. Sites like Kickstarter or Indiegogo allow you to contribute $1, $25, $1,000—whatever you want—to an exciting business or project idea. While you don't get any of your money back, you might get a perk like a branded shopping bag or water bottle. Some beer companies name new beers after their top donors. Because donations are not regarded as "securities," these sites are largely unregulated. There are now literally thousands of these donation sites on the Internet and they attract billions of dollars in mostly local donations every year.[6]

The second flavor of crowdfunding is interest-free lending to businesses. The best example is Kiva, which allows you to find great microentrepreneurs around the world, learn about their businesses, and help them get started and grow. Because loans without interest also are not regarded as securities, this kind of lending has proliferated as well. Again, you might get some perks from your loan, in addition to getting your principal back, but the main satisfaction is personal. If you find an entrepreneur in your community, you will also enjoy a social return from the business's success.

The third flavor of crowdfunding is peer-to-peer lending. Sites like Prosper and LendingClub provide individuals and businesses the opportunity to borrow as much as $35,000–$40,000 from small investors. These lending platforms pay interest rates of about 10 percent these days, though the loans are risky. The problem for a local investor, however, is that you can see only the state in which the borrowers live. The community location is hidden.

The fourth flavor is what Title III of the JOBS Act of 2012 legalized and is often called "investment crowdfunding." Small businesses can put up an offering on a federally licensed portal, like Wefunder, and you can invest as much as $2,200 per year (or more if your income is over $107,000).

Introduced by Tea Party Republicans, with the enthusiastic support of young techies and local-economy advocates like myself, the JOBS Act created an affordable, legal pathway for small businesses to get investment capital from any American. Unlike donation crowdfunding, investment crowdfunding allows businesses to borrow money from their fans and pay them interest. Or sell them stock and pay dividends. Or provide royalty payments on revenues or profits. Or enter into dozens of other kinds of investment arrangements. Now everyone can play in the sandbox of business finance, not just rich people. Small businesses can seek grassroots investors, and grassroots investors can put their money into small businesses.

According to the most recent assessment of investment crowdfunding, between 2017 and 2018 the number of unique offerings grew from 474 to 680, the annual total raised increased from $71 million to $109 million, and the number of investors rose from 77,558 to 147,448.[7] Six in ten companies that tried crowdfunding succeeded, with an average raise of $270,966.

These numbers will grow, but in the larger scheme of things, this revolution is still a mouse. Of the 330 million people living in the United States, fewer than one in a thousand have participated in crowdfunding. There are lots of explanations why. News travels slowly. People resist change. Novel concepts need time to prove themselves. But the most significant explanation, I believe, is quite specific: The only real savings most of us have—the dollars we might be able to invest locally—are locked away in our pension funds, IRAs, and 401ks. And if we have bothered to ask about other options, we have been told by our financial advisors and other experts that local investment is impossible within these accounts.

This advice is wrong. Most advisors are unaware of recent changes in the law that have expanded local investment options. Nor are they familiar with the tax tools for tapping retirement funds for local investment that have been available for decades. This book is all about two of the most important tools: the Self-Directed IRA and the Solo 401k. While there are differences between the two, they are sufficiently similar to be discussed together in one book. I call them, for simplicity, Do-It-Yourself (DIY) Accounts.

If you've ever listened to experts talking about these tools, you may have heard them say, "The Self-Directed IRA is really expensive." "The Solo 401k is too complicated." "Finding companies that offer these products is way too difficult."

These pronouncements pile on top of the other commonly heard refrain: "Don't bother investing in local businesses, because they usually fail." As we will discuss later, this is all ill-informed nonsense.

All investment is risky, whether you invest in Wall Street or Main Street. But if you approach local investment with prudence and common sense, you can earn a rate of return that matches or exceeds what you would get on the stock market, while being sure your money is supporting your community and your local economy. This book aims to give you all the basic information you need to open your own DIY Accounts and to start investing locally.

While I've tried to write a book that's informative, interesting, and occasionally entertaining, my mission is not just to provide a good read. I want you to act. *I want you to make a commitment to start moving your money back into your life.*

To help you follow through, I have teamed up with the Sustainable Economies Law Center and LIFT Economy to create a website, called The Next Egg (*www.thenextegg.org*), that puts all the tools you need in one place. Through webinars, reports, peer support, and specific services, The Next Egg can help you unlock everything you read about in the pages that follow.

I've written this book for people without a lot of investment experience. I explain in simple terms concepts like "liquidity" and "diversification" that often sound complicated but are not. If you already know a lot about investment, you'll be able to skim some sections. But even if you are as experienced as Warren Buffett, I invite you to rethink everything you know about the field. How might you bring more meaning and satisfaction to the deployment of your money?

The book begins with some examples of how the DIY Accounts work (Chapter 1). It then proceeds to describe the importance of local business (Chapter 2), introduce the field of local investment (Chapter 3), and present a dozen specific kinds of local investment options (Chapter 4)—some of which are very likely to generate better returns than Wall Street. The rest of the book introduces everything you need to know about Self-Directed IRAs and Solo 401ks. Here are the questions these remaining chapters seek to answer:

- What are the basics of the DIY Accounts? (Chapter 5)
- How do you set up a DIY Account? (Chapter 6)
- How do you begin identifying local investment opportunities? (Chapter 7)
- How should you evaluate these opportunities? (Chapter 8)
- How can you prevent yourself from swimming in legally dangerous waters? (Chapter 9)
- How do you keep your DIY Account operating successfully? (Chapter 10)
- What's happening next in the field of local investment? (Chapter 11)

Here are a few caveats before we proceed:

- Any honest book about investment needs to dispel the fantasy that you are going to get rich quick. Instead, I repeat this warning: *Any investment, even a local investment, carries risk.* And while this book provides you with tools and strategies for conducting due diligence and making smart investment decisions, you should still try to get other informed opinions before committing your precious savings. There are plenty of other great books out there designed specifically to sharpen your investment skills.

- You also might consult the other books that have been published on Self-Directed IRAs and Solo 401ks—as you will see in the notes and resources—though none focus on local investment per se. They all delve more deeply into the legal fine print. If you are interested in using your DIY Account to invest in special kinds of opportunities not linked to your community—like housing liens or precious metals—please consult these books and other experts for guidance on how to do so.

- This book is not a legal textbook, and consequently I won't bore you with extensive explanations on whether this or that rule comes from a piece of legislation, an IRS ruling, or case law. As a lawyer, I've tried to capture the essence of the law, regulations, and court holdings in plain language. For those who are eager to learn more about these questions, I've added notes.

- Please be mindful of the 2020 publication date. Laws and regulations concerning taxes, pension savings, and investment always change, and huge overhauls are always possible. If you happen to pick up this book in 2021 or later, please double-check The Next Egg website for updates.

- Finally, I want to give a special, supportive shout-out to the hundreds of thousands of professionals currently working in the financial industry. I know that most of you are trying to do your best to serve the needs of customers to protect and grow their savings. Even though I'm critical of some of the industry's practices, I hope you won't take these criticisms personally. Instead, I would like you, too, to see the fabulous new opportunities to incorporate the tools and practices of local investment into your business. Change is hard, but in your case, it also could be enormously profitable.

Okay, enough throat clearing. Let's get on with your new life as a local investor!

1

PUTTING YOUR MONEY IN YOUR LIFE

Local investment may sound exotic, but opportunities for putting your savings to work in your community are becoming more common and more lucrative. At this point, most authors of investment books will spin stories that show their financial brilliance. Here's how I transformed powdered moose antlers into a $100 million health-food empire! Instead, I will tell you an embarrassing story of my own short-sightedness that almost drove me into bankruptcy. If I knew then what I know now, I could have prevented more than a decade of serious financial struggle. My mistake, however, is now your opportunity.

One of my favorite Gary Larson cartoons is of a crisis clinic on fire, floating down a river, about to plunge over a waterfall. That's what my life was like in 2008. That was the year I had decided to divorce, start paying child support for two young children, move into a new house, and take a new job. Then the financial crisis hit. My new job vanished, and opportunities for consulting work were drying up. Having been married to a talented law professor with an expertise in family law—please don't laugh—I was struggling to keep up with punishing custody payments and lawyer bills.

The one financial bright spot was that my spouse had accumulated a significant pension, and we agreed, as part of our divorce settlement, that half would be transferred to me. Normally, you cannot touch tax-deferred funds like these until you retire, and if you do, you will be sacked by the Internal Revenue Service (IRS) with a 10 percent penalty. But when a court orders the redistribution of marital assets, you can use them immediately without penalty. Ordinary taxes are taken out of money you withdraw, and then the funds are yours. I decided to use the proceeds to pay off all my debts—credit cards, automobile, various personal loans. I thought it would be smart to begin my new life with a clean financial slate.

About a year later, as I was doing my taxes, I learned something the divorce attorneys never warned me about. The transfer of funds pushed me into a substantially higher income bracket, and the much-dreaded alternative minimum tax kicked in. Suddenly I owed Uncle Sam about $80,000. I paid off some of this debt with credit cards, and the rest went into an IRS payment plan. After paying over 20 percent interest and penalties for several years, my debt situation was far worse than it had been before I divorced!

I have since learned about an option that could have saved me all this grief. A Solo 401k is a retirement savings account designed for self-employed individuals, which is what I was in 2009. I could have transferred my former wife's pension into that account and given myself a five-year, $50,000 loan to pay off all my debts. There would never have been an awful tax bill from the IRS. In fact, no taxes would have been taken out of the transfer at all, because I would have rolled it over directly into another tax-deferred account. And instead of paying over 20 percent interest to credit card companies for years, I could have paid my Solo 401k back at 5 percent interest over five years, and the literally tens of thousands of dollars of interest I had paid to Visa and Mastercard would have instead gone straight into my retirement account. Rather than being broke with massive debts in front of me, I would have paid everything off in five years and had a healthy nest egg for retirement. Smart local investing in myself would have paid huge dividends.

Okay, I was a fool. But then again, no one in my life—not my lawyers, not financial advisors I consulted, not my many Ivy League–educated friends—knew about the Solo 401k either. Neither did you, I bet. Live and learn. You, however, will never have to repeat this mistake. Because I'm now about to introduce you to the huge, unappreciated potential of DIY Accounts.

Right now, chances are good that your life savings are locked away in Individual Retirement Accounts (IRAs) and their workplace equivalents (401ks or 403bs). The government incentivizes you to maximize your retirement savings in these accounts by deferring taxes until you withdraw the money in retirement. Unfortunately, your investment options in these accounts are almost entirely global corporations. But with the Self-Directed IRA (which anyone can use) or the Solo 401k (which is designed for self-employed people), you can save for your retirement, defer your taxes, and invest locally.

Local investment means putting your money to work in your local businesses, your community, your neighbors, and even yourself. We can quibble about whether your community is your region, your town, or your neighborhood, but for the moment let's underscore one basic truth: The closer to home you invest, the more benefits you are likely to enjoy and the more informed you will be about the risks.

Let me give you some hypothetical examples of what local investment looks like and how the Self-Directed IRA and Solo 401k can unlock its full potential.

- George is a forty-year-old software engineer who has steadily put away $5,000 per year in his IRA. He has accumulated about $80,000 and manages his investments online through TD Ameritrade. He worries that all his money is supporting Fortune 500 businesses he knows little about, and he now wants to put some of that money into his local food cooperative. The co-op, which has operated for twenty years, is building another store and is prepared to pay members 7 percent per year for loans above $1,000. George decides to set up a Self-Directed IRA through PENSCO Trust, one of several dozen companies that provide this tool, and directs his appointed representative, called his "custodian," to lend the co-op $10,000. The note from his IRA is payable over five years, and every year the co-op pays $2,495 back into his IRA. The cost of setting this up? About $250 per year.

- Ashley is thirty and has a smaller IRA than George. She has a friend who is launching a nearby clothing business and is crowdfunding on the website Honeycomb Credit for the $250,000 she needs in start-up capital. Ashley also sets up a Self-Directed IRA, rolls over funds from her original IRA, and then directs her custodian to write a $2,000 check to Honeycomb Credit. She now is thrilled that she—along with 550 other people—has loaned her friend's company the capital it needs to get going.

- Maureen, fifty, is excited about a new museum dedicated to local civil rights activism. Her city has issued municipal bonds to support the museum, but instead of selling the bonds through Wall Street investment banks, it is encouraging residents to buy the bonds directly. According to the mayor, "We are promoting local investment because it's giving the city a new tool for underwriting municipal projects without raising taxes." Maureen sets up a Self-Directed IRA, rolls over her savings, and buys $5,000 worth of bonds.

- Ken, thirty-eight and single, has been a self-employed musician. He barely has been making ends meet, but this past year, he recorded a single that's getting wide play on YouTube and SiriusXM. Six months of wildly successful concerts have netted him $196,000, significantly more than he needs for expenses. He decides to set up a Solo 401k and place his maximum annual contribution, $56,000, into it. Instead of paying roughly $44,000 in taxes on $196,000 worth of income, he pays only $26,000 on $140,000.[1] Since it's a Solo 401k, he doesn't need to hire a custodian. Instead, he purchases a license to an agreement from the IRS called a "prototype" from a trust company and uses it to govern a new account he sets up in the name of his Solo 401k at his own bank. At a cost of about $300 per year, he can be his own custodian. A self-proclaimed "solar enthusiast," he then invests in a half-dozen promising renewable energy projects around his city.

- Robin has worked for the Foreign Service all her life and has steadily built up a million dollars in her Thrift Savings Plan (TSP), the federal government's equivalent of a 401k. Her investment options, when she was working for the federal government, were mostly global stocks and bonds. When she decides to retire at fifty-six, she sets up her own online knitting business. After she sells her first piece and reports that income on Schedule C of her taxes, she opens up a Solo 401k. She then directs her TSP representative to transfer the million dollars into her Solo account, and she begins to invest in affordable housing projects in her community.

- Robin's neighbor, Gwen, came over for dinner and shared the awful news that she had breast cancer, had been slammed by huge medical bills, and recently had racked up $25,000 in credit card debt. She was practically in tears, not knowing how she would ever pay it back with annual interest rates over 20 percent. Robin said, "Look, I can help. Right now, I've got $25,000 in retirement savings sitting in my bank and earning about 2 percent interest per year. How about I pay off your credit card, and then you pay me back at 5 percent per year over the next five years? You can write me into your life insurance for collateral." Robin uses her Solo 401k, enters into an agreement with Gwen on behalf of her account, and then cuts her the $25,000 check.

All these examples show how anyone can take money sitting in a tax-deferred account and use DIY Accounts to reinvest it locally. Investing locally, of course, doesn't mean the investments will pay off as promised. With any investment, whether local or not, the people mentioned here—George, Ashley, Maureen, Ken, and Robin—could lose everything. But local investing gave these people an opportunity to put their money in people, projects, and businesses they really cared about. And it gave them the potential of generating higher returns with lower risks than the typical Wall Street stocks and bonds.

Local Milk and Beyond in Washington State

"I thought it was important to move our money from Wall Street and get our money back into our local community," says Judith Culver of Bellingham, Washington, who set up a Self-Directed Roth IRA with New Standard IRA in 2011. The lowest start-up fee she could find was $1,300 but she has paid only $80 per year since. She joined a local investment club that has helped her think through her investment decisions.

Her first investment was a $15,000 loan to a local dairy processing company so it could add a bottling facility. "This was at a time when it was really difficult for people to get money from the conventional banking system," recounts Judith. By bypassing Wall Street, she reasoned, she could foster economic growth in her own community.

"We went to the farm twice, learning about the baby calves [and] the milking as we sat and ate zucchini bread with the business owner," Judith says. The farmer was so adamant about paying her back that he said, "I would put this in my will if I could."

Her investment did well, paying her returns of about 6 to 12 percent per year. She decided to make another loan to a local business focused on a food distribution network for local farmers. That investment also did well. And she followed with investments in a local wind farm, a local author (who needed funds to publish his book on community yoga), and a local manufacturer of ergonomic chairs.

As far as Judith is concerned, New Standard made the process very easy. But her local investment group was invaluable as well in helping her find local investment opportunities.

2

CARING ABOUT LOCAL

You have heard me use the word "local" nearly fifty times so far in this book—local investment, local business, local economies—and you're probably wondering what it means. How exactly do I define "local"? Why should we care about it? Isn't anything that makes money a worthwhile investment, independent of place?

What's a Good Definition of "Local"?

The term "local" embodies not one but three distinct concepts—proximity, ownership, and control. When people talk about local food, they often mean that the distance from the farm to your kitchen table is short. Proximity matters because you can get to know—and trust—all the people who touch your food along the way. Proximity means a lower carbon footprint for a purchase, if you're worried about climate change. It means more local self-reliance and resilience, if you're worried about far-away threats like mad cow disease or getting your oil supply cut off.

"Local" also refers to local ownership. Suppose your community has a factory manufacturing refrigerators and selling them to the world. If that factory is locally owned, it's far less likely to move to China and take away local jobs. It's also more likely to buy supplies locally, which increases its contribution to community well-being. We know that locally owned businesses tend to re-spend more of their money locally—on local accountants and lawyers, on local advertising, in local profits—and these expenditures multiply through the regional economy in the form of more income, wealth, and jobs. More on this "multiplier effect" shortly.

For a community to enjoy all the benefits of a given business, however, that business not only needs to be locally owned but also locally controlled. Think about franchises. A McDonald's restaurant might be locally owned, but technically, the franchise holder can't buy supplies locally, can't design his own signage, and can't advertise freely—behaviors that might otherwise increase the positive economic impacts for the community.

Given these considerations, I define a local business as one where 51 percent or more of the owners live in the community where the business operates, and where the key business decisions are locally controlled. But we still might quibble about the right size of a community. Is it a neighborhood? A city? A county? A metropolitan area? A region? Probably the best answer is "it depends." Multiplier benefits are usually stronger over shorter distances, but residents sometimes relate more deeply to larger places.

As an investor, you might focus on a different question: How well do you know the business, project, or person you are investing in? Knowledge is key for developing trust and avoiding fraud. Usually, the closer the investment is to where you live, the easier it is to develop this kind of relationship. Is the business close enough to visit, to try out the good or service, to meet the management team? With these questions in mind, a regional framework for "local" might be fine.

Businesses come in an alphabet soup of legal structures, and almost any of them can be locally owned. It can be an informal, sole proprietorship. It can be a C Corp, an S Corp, or a B Corp. It can be a consumer-owned or worker-owned cooperative. It can even be a nonprofit (though technically no one owns a nonprofit) if the board overseeing it lives locally. In fact, over 96 percent of all business entities in the United States are locally owned![1] This is because tens of millions of sole proprietorships account for nearly all the businesses in America.

The only kinds of companies that are clearly not local are those you are probably invested in now—publicly traded companies like Home Depot, Merck, and Microsoft. Walmart is not locally owned or controlled anywhere, except by its shareholders, who live all over the world. Even Walmart's managers living at the home base in Bentonville, Arkansas, ultimately must answer to these far-flung stock owners.

Mainstream financial institutions pooh-pooh locally owned businesses as not worthy of their and your attention. But one unappreciated fact about locally owned businesses is that they are responsible for most of the jobs and output in the US economy.[2] One in ten working Americans are sole proprietors, many running home-based businesses. One in five work in very small businesses with one to ninety-nine employees. About three in ten are in medium-scale businesses with ninety-nine to five hundred employees. Nearly all these businesses are locally owned. The only real category for nonlocal businesses is businesses that have more than five hundred employees—and those businesses represent about 40 percent of the economy, by jobs and output. It's also worth pointing out that plenty of very large companies, like hospitals or universities, are locally owned as well. Thus, while almost all small businesses are locally owned, not all locally owned businesses are small.

The private company Dun & Bradstreet, which maintains an updated inventory of every business establishment in the country, has a slightly different definition of "local." It calls an establishment—an office, a factory, a store—local if its headquarters is in the same state. By that definition, about 80 percent of the economy in the United States, again by jobs and output, is locally owned.[3]

So, depending on the definition of "local," locally owned businesses are responsible for 60–80 percent of the US economy. And in a well-functioning investment marketplace, 60–80 percent of your money should be supporting 60–80 percent of the economy. Today, almost none is.

The good news is that there are plenty of local companies in which you can invest. Tens of millions, in fact! And remember that local investment doesn't have to be in a business. Every person you know and care about in your community is a potentially promising recipient of local investment as well.

But let's continue to focus, for the moment, on local business.

Loving Local Business in Michigan

For Cathy Muha, a retiree in Michigan, her Self-Directed IRA has helped her not only to align her finances with her values but also to give her a fuller life as she keeps her finger on the pulse of the local businesses she loves. She has been helped along the way by Angela Barbash, a registered investment advisor who leads a firm called Revalue. (We will learn more about Angela's work later in the book.) Angela guided Cathy through the paperwork and found promising Michigan companies for her to invest in.

Cathy made an equity investment in a "farm stop" called Agricole in her own town, Chelsea. It's like a farmers' market, only indoors and open all year. It features produce and prepared items from local sources. "I love that it helps local farmers and producers and gives me access to fresh, often organic foods. It's also a bit of a gathering place, with a small cafe and coffee shop." Agricole is an L3C, meaning it's a low-profit, limited liability company. Cathy doesn't expect to make much money off of this investment but is excited about her social return—that "it's contributing to the health and well-being of the community."

Another one of her investments is in Unity Vibration, an award-winning kombucha company located in nearby Ypsilanti. "I love Ypsilanti," Cathy says, "It's a town with people who have been pulling themselves up for quite a while, and I'm really happy to be able to support them."

A third company Cathy invested in is the Michigan Farm Market, a small northern Michigan prepared-foods company specializing in cheesecakes that was started by Scotty Bruce, who neatly delivers local food in delightful packages. Before she invested $10,000, she met with Scotty over dinner and learned about his story and passion. "It's just fun not only to know where your money is, but with whom your money is. These are passionate people. You're pulling for them, not just because your money is there but because they're good people."

Another company in Cathy's portfolio is City Girls in Pontiac, Michigan. The company uses goat milk to create lotions and soaps. Through her Self-Directed IRA, Cathy loaned City Girls enough money to buy a school bus to transport the goats to different fields where the goats could "mow down" invasive species and also get the nutrition required to produce high-quality milk for City Girls' products. Before Cathy invested, she made a trip to Pontiac, and part of her due diligence was coping with a goat nibbling on her scarf and jacket.

While she says this form of investing isn't the easiest, she still recommends it to her friends, saying the complexity is worth it. "Moving your money from point A to point B to point C can be complicated. You have to do it right to make sure it doesn't get taxed." She compared the process to the game she played as a child, hopping from couch to couch to avoid touching the ground.

Cathy can easily check the status of her investments online and continues to rely on Revalue Investing to help her with her choices. "You don't want to be the only one vetting the businesses," she advises.

"I'm not out to earn the biggest bang for my buck," says Cathy. "I do want to earn something, but that's not the most important thing to me. Putting my money where my conscience is is what is most important to me right now."

Why Should We Care about the Ownership of a Business?

If you have two possible investments, one a locally owned business and one not, identical in terms of their expected risk and returns, you should always favor the local investment. Why? Because with the local investment, you not only get the same private rate of return but you also enjoy a *social* return. A new local business, fortified with your investment, means more local hires, who pay more taxes, which allows your local government to employ more teachers and police, which improves the quality of *your* life. It's a virtuous cycle. And even though we don't know exactly how to quantify all these social benefits, we know they are not zero. In fact, most of us regard quality of life, including quality of schools, level of crime, and presence of parks and amenities, as the principal driver for our decisions about where to live. As Dorothy reminds us in *The Wizard of Oz*, "There's no place like home."

Local businesses turn out to be the key to community prosperity and success. Again, a local business spends more in the local economy—it imparts a more profound "multiplier effect" than a nonlocal business.

Over the past twenty years, about two dozen studies have compared the impacts of local versus similar nonlocal businesses and found that the local businesses generate two to four times the jobs and other economic-development impacts. Many of these studies have been prepared by Matt Cunningham and Dan Houston, two economists running Civic Economics in Austin, Texas. Its most recent study, from 2019, compares the economic impacts of Central Co-op in Seattle with similarly sized chain grocery stores.[4] For every dollar of sales, Central Co-op recirculates forty-eight cents, almost double what is re-spent by a competing chain. The higher spending by the Co-op is driven by having a more labor-intensive business, paying its workers more, procuring more local foodstuffs, and giving more to local charities. If the Co-op were replaced by another chain grocer, the Seattle economy would lose eighty-two jobs because of the lower multiplier effects.

There's a growing body of evidence that regions with higher densities of local businesses have superior economic performance and that economic-development strategies that emphasize the nurturing of local businesses perform better than those that focus on attracting big, global companies.[5] For example,

- A 2010 study appeared in *Harvard Business Review* under the headline "More Small Firms Means More Jobs."[6] The authors wrote, "Our research shows that regional economic growth is highly correlated with the presence of many small, entrepreneurial employers—not a few big ones." They further argued that the major pre-occupation of economic developers, namely how to attract global companies with subsidies, is fundamentally wrongheaded. "Politicians enjoy announcing a big company's arrival because people tend to think that will mean lots of job openings. But in a rapidly evolving economy, politicians are all too likely to guess wrong about which industries are worth attracting. What's more, large corporations often generate little employment growth even if they are doing well."

- Another study published shortly thereafter in the *Economic Development Quarterly*, a journal long supportive of business-attraction practices, similarly found that "economic growth models that control for other relevant factors reveal a positive relationship between density of locally owned firms and per capita income growth, but only for small firms (ten to ninety-nine employees), whereas the density of large firms (more than five hundred workers) not owned locally has a negative effect."[7] Put in plain English, if you want higher wages, focus on local businesses.

- That's the message of a paper published in 2013 by the Federal Reserve in Atlanta, which analyzed counties across the United States and found statistically significant "evidence that local entrepreneurship matters for local economic performance. . . . The percent of employment provided by resident, or locally-owned, business establishments has a significant positive effect on county income and employment growth and a significant and negative effect on poverty."[8]

- A study published in 2018 by the Upjohn Institute for Employment Research, another institution that has historically published studies offering qualified support for the use of subsidies to attract big outside businesses, compared the economic-development achievements of jurisdictions that deploy attraction "incentives" with those that focus instead on nurturing local businesses. "When we examine the overall effectiveness of state incentive grants on firm-level performance, we find little evidence that they generate new jobs and other direct economic benefits to the states that employ them."[9]

Local businesses contribute to a strong community in other ways as well. My earlier books—*Going Local* (1998); *The Small-Mart Revolution* (2006); *Local Dollars, Local Sense* (2012); and *The Local Economy Solution* (2015)—elaborated these arguments, but I'll summarize them here.

Local ownership of business stabilizes an economy. A community with one big factory, run by outsiders, is extremely vulnerable to decisions made in boardrooms hundreds or thousands of miles away. As many single-company locales in the United States have learned—especially those producing resource-dependent products like fish, paper, wood, oil, or coal—if a global corporation takes over the home company and decides it can get a slightly higher return by moving its plant elsewhere, perhaps to Mexico or Vietnam, the community can collapse overnight. A community with a diversity of local businesses, in contrast, will be able to adapt gradually to inevitable changes in the national and global economy. While a global factory owner will move from place to place, looking for the highest rate of return, a local factory owner may be happy to stay if the factory is generating even a small but positive rate of return.

The greater economic stability of communities filled with local businesses means greater employee loyalty and less mobility.[10] In 1946, two noted social scientists, C. Wright Mills and Melville Ulmer, explored this question by comparing communities dominated by a couple of large manufacturers versus those communities characterized by large numbers of small businesses. They found that small-business communities "provided for their residents a considerably more balanced economic life than did big business cities" and that "the general level of civic welfare was appreciably higher."[11] Thomas Lyson, a professor of rural sociology at Cornell, updated this study in 2001 by looking at 226 manufacturing-dependent counties in the United States. His conclusion was that these communities are "vulnerable to greater inequality, lower levels of welfare, and increased rates of social disruption than localities where the economy is more diversified."[12]

We know that the deeper the roots residents have in a community, the more likely they are to vote, and that economically diverse communities have higher participation rates in local politics. Harvard political scientist Robert Putnam has identified these long-term relationships in stable communities as facilitating the kinds of civic institutions—schools, churches, charities, fraternal leagues, business clubs—that are essential for economic success. Reviewing the broader social science literature on the relationship of local businesses to civil society, another group of scholars concluded, "The degree to which the economic underpinnings of local communities can be stabilized—or not—will be inextricably linked with the quality of American democracy in the coming century."[13]

Rootedness contributes to quality of life. One study found evidence that counties characterized by a greater density of local businesses have less crime and better public health.[14] The authors who made this finding surmise that the social connections and greater wealth of these communities contribute to more effective collective decision-making. Recent research on food systems has shown that local business communities, by embracing local food that's fresher and less processed, have lower rates of obesity and type 2 diabetes.[15]

Another sign of a community's health is how well it preserves its unique culture, foods, ecology, architecture, history, music, and art. By definition, local businesses, especially local retailers, are likely to carry that local DNA. "A retail environment not indicative of 'anywhere America,'" one study concludes, "help[s] those able to move to be less prone to feel that they could replace their current place of residence with anywhere else in America."[16] Put another way, community pride convinces the best and brightest to stick around. Richard Florida argues that the "creative class" is drawn to local business communities that celebrate civic culture.[17] So are tourists, who are especially attracted to restaurants, shops, and museums that are unique signatures of a community. A growing number of communities are engaged in a strategy of "placemaking," promoted by groups like Main Street America and the Project for Public Spaces, which activate plazas, parks, blocks, districts, and neighborhoods by spreading locally owned businesses.

Sustainability also is served by local businesses. By definition, a world of communities that each maximize their reliance on the sustainable use of locally renewable resources will place fewer demands on other communities' resources. Every innovation in a community that increases local resilience—a geothermal heating project, greenhouses that supply fresh local food all year long, apartment buildings that use local timber—provides a working model, if shared, for other communities worldwide to deploy. A community that's self-reliant also has less need to import things, which brings down the carbon footprint. A community with a diversity of local businesses and more self-reliance can have more control over its destiny. Moreover, because the owners of local businesses are part of the community, they tend to act more responsibly. A study from the EPA has shown that when you compare two similar factories, one locally owned and one not, the locally owned factory generates about a tenth as much pollution.[18]

The Bottom Line

The goal of any community eager to become more prosperous should be to start, nurture, and expand local businesses. Local businesses are the key to economic development. Compared to similarly sized global businesses, they spend more money locally, pump up the economic multiplier more powerfully, and create more income, wealth, and jobs. They also happen to be great for promoting local social stability, tourism, charitable giving, resilience, and sustainability. Local investment gives you and your neighbors the ability to become the most important economic developers in your community.

3

INVESTING LOCALLY

Local investors seek to maximize both their social rate of return and their personal rate of return, while keeping risks to a minimum. Many worry, however, that local companies generate smaller returns than global companies. And they have been told by financial advisors they trust that most local businesses fail. Both concerns, we shall see, are incorrect. But another concern is very real. The entire field of local investment is immature, and the institutions that make global investment easy largely do not exist yet at the local level. So smart local investment—for the moment—requires significant work.

Are Local Businesses Less Profitable than Global Companies? Riskier?

Strong and weak companies come in all sizes. Many large and small companies are highly profitable, and many large and small companies suddenly go out of business. The challenge for any investor, global or local, is to pick wisely. But are there larger patterns that can inform these choices?

Indeed, there are! And not a few of you will be surprised to learn that smaller companies are *more* profitable than big ones. The most recent data from the Internal Revenue Service (IRS), from the year 2013, show that sole proprietorships, which most small businesses are or start out as, are three times more profitable than C Corporations, with the profitability of partnerships falling in between.[1] In our not wildly dissimilar neighbor to the north, Canada, the most current data suggest that the most profitable companies have ten to twenty employees, while the least profitable are the largest, with more than five hundred employees.[2]

Walking the Talk in North Carolina

In the universe of local investment pioneers, Carol Peppe Hewitt is a star. She has built a strong network of local investors in North Carolina, prototyped microloans to entrepreneurs across the state, and written about it in her book, *Financing Our Foodshed: Growing Local Food with Slow Money* (New Society, 2013). After having facilitated hundreds of thousands of dollars in microlending to farmers and local food businesses in the state, she discovered the Self-Directed IRA. She set one up to help her friend Mary start a rabbit farm with a $5,000 loan.

Carol worked through a company called Equity Trust, which now serves as the custodian for her account. She had shopped around and looked at several companies but decided to go with Equity Trust because it charged a flat annual fee rather than a per-transaction fee.

One reason Mary was the right choice for an initial investment was that she had an accounting background. Carol intuited that the process might require that she and Mary both do some homework to test out this kind of investment. She was right.

"Putting the money in wasn't a big deal," she says, "setting it up wasn't a big deal, but making a loan out of it was a big deal. The forms are tricky, and you have to get every single thing right. . . . It's time consuming." To make a loan, she had to prepare a promissory note for Equity Trust, which required her to work closely with Mary and notarize the documents.

"I could have just loaned her the money," Carol admits, "but I wanted to practice using these tools because I think they're important."

In well-functioning capital marketplaces, higher profit rates of return for small businesses should translate into higher rates of return for local investors. The problem right now, however, is that the marketplace for local investments is immature.

In a mature marketplace, like the one that has developed over the last century around big businesses, there are professionals who help you find promising investments, evaluate them, trade them, put them into funds, and connect them with your retirement accounts. These professionals barely exist in the local investment universe, so you have to do more of this work yourself. This is changing—more and more finance professionals are reading books like this and rethinking their business models—but for now the burden is on you.

What about risk? If you were to ask a typical investment advisor what she thought about your taking some of your money and putting it into a bookstore you love, she would probably say something like, "You're crazy! You'll never get your money back. Most small businesses fail."

Your advisor just made a surprisingly common mistake, conflating all small businesses with small business *startups*. Your bookstore, it turns out, has been around for twenty years, has an excellent track record of profitability, and wants to do a modest expansion—it's not a startup. All startups, big and small, nonlocal and local, have a high failure rate. Most don't survive past five years or so. *But well over 90 percent of all small businesses are not startups.* If you are risk averse, the key is not to stay away from local businesses but to stay away from startups.

That's not to say, however, that investing in proven local businesses is without risk. Your bookstore's expansion plan could be a dud. Amazon might have a plan for a new popup store across the street. And there are some special risks posed by local investment that are worth paying attention to. If you continued the conversation with your investment advisor, she would probably give you at least four other reasons not to invest in even existing local businesses. Pay attention to all of them:

- *Limited Investors*—If you're a business looking exclusively for local investors, it's going to be harder for you to find them. Compared to the universe of Wall Street investors, the universe of investors in your community is tiny.

- *Limited Businesses*—If you're an investor looking exclusively for local companies, you will have fewer options to choose from, and your chance of choosing wrong is greater.

- *Geographic Risk*—Every regional economy naturally goes through ups and downs. If your investment portfolio is made up exclusively of local business and your region goes through a recession, your losses may be more extreme. That's why some investment advisors believe that, at a minimum, your portfolio might have locally owned businesses from different places.

- *Limited Information*—When you want to invest in a Wall Street company, you can go to Google Finance or hundreds of other data providers and get key facts about companies before investing in them. If you are a professional investor, you might buy special analytical reports from companies like Moody's. Right now, there are no uniform reports you can obtain about local companies.

Again, on all these points your investment advisor is right. But your reaction should be caution, not fear. And curiosity.

If your advisor were to give you the complete picture, she would go on and tell you the ways in which local investing also can *reduce* your risk.

- *Better Information*—Even though there are not formal information sources about local business, you can find most of the information you need. You can walk into the business, pose questions to the manager, and kibitz with the workforce. You can ground truth what you think about the company's products or services. Frankly, it turns out this is the best way of evaluating companies anyway. We know this because community banks with long relationships with companies have lower default rates than global banks that rely strictly on computer-generated credit scores.

- *Social Returns*—Remember that a local business delivers both a private return and a community (or social) return. Unlike a nonlocal investment, there are multiple ways a local investment can benefit you. Even if the company doesn't deliver much of a profit to you personally, you still will enjoy the benefits of a stronger local economy, cleaner streets, better schools, and so forth. We can argue about how much weight to give this return, but it's something.

- *Local Synergies*—A third advantage of local investment is the opportunities it presents for new investment strategies. Remember the risk of geographic concentration? It's real but there's a flip side. Your portfolio can enjoy potential synergies if it contains interconnected local companies. If you invest in an established restaurant that puts its second eatery in an otherwise dead downtown, that new business might bring the foot traffic that will help every other new business in that area succeed. A smart local investor might invest in the restaurant *and* the movie theater next store *and* the coffee house across the street. And if you wanted to be mindful of the risks of geographic concentration, you might invest like this in multiple downtowns across the country.

- *Increased Diversification*—The idea behind having a diversified portfolio of investments is if one fails, the others will be unscathed. We want our investments to be different enough so that they cannot fail in the same way, at the same time, or because of some common cause. The essential problem with your portfolio right now is that almost everything in it—stocks, bonds, commercial paper, mutual funds, even currencies—is tied to the performance of global companies. A trade war, a global capital crisis, the collapse of major currencies will adversely affect everything in your portfolio. Truly local investments, in contrast, are somewhat more insulated.

But there is one additional risk inherent in local investing that you need to be aware of, because it dictates how a smart investor needs to approach today.

What's the State of the Local Investment Marketplace?

Inchoate. Spotty. Full of potholes.

Think about the investment universe that exists today with the world's biggest companies. Thousands of publicly traded companies have issued stocks and bonds that wel-come investments from grassroots investors. Grassroots investors can buy these stocks and bonds individually and then resell them on various stock exchanges. Or they can put their money into index funds, pension funds, or mutual funds that hold various kinds of stocks and bonds. And the law permits anyone with an IRA or a 401k to invest tax-deferred dollars into any of these opportunities.

Very few of these investment institutions exist yet for local investors. Only a tiny number of small businesses wel-come grassroots investors, despite recent changes in the law. For small businesses that issue stock for grassroots investors, there are almost no institutions like Moody's or Standard & Poor's to evaluate them and give investors confidence they won't be swindled. There are also no local stock exchanges to facilitate the trading of local stocks and bonds. Without transparent trading mechanisms, it's hard to know exactly what these investments are worth. Funds that hold invest-ments without clear valuations have difficulty attracting investors. This is one explanation of why so few funds exist for local investors (though their numbers are expanding). And the types of IRAs and 401ks offered to most investors now make it challenging to move funds into any local busi-nesses or local investment funds.

The absence of these institutions means that a local inves-tor today has to spend more time, effort, and even money to do smart investing. And once the investment is made, the investor has a tougher time getting out of the investment. In the professional lingo, many local investments are not very "liquid." Some students of the stock market argue that half or more of the "price" of stocks is not for a share of the company per se but for the right to resell that share any day, any time, to anyone.

The good news is that the local versions of these institutions are beginning to emerge. And in a decade or two, there *will* be many local brokerages, local investment advisors, local securities evaluators, local stock exchanges, and local mutual funds. As archaic securities laws get updated, as word spreads about local opportunities, as examples of local investing success multiply, these innovations are almost guaranteed. Where there are markets for new kinds of investment, finance entrepreneurs will appear to take advantage of these opportunities. That's capitalism at its best.

But before we get into specifics of how to invest locally, it's worth pausing for a moment and reflecting on how we got here. How did we wind up with a system that rewards big businesses rather than the small and medium businesses that make up most of our economy?

What's Wrong with the Capital Marketplace?

According to regular reports put out by the Federal Reserve, Americans now have about $13.8 trillion sitting in banks and $56.5 trillion in stocks, bonds, pension funds, mutual funds, and insurance funds.[3] If the investment marketplace were operating properly, between 60 and 80 percent of these investment dollars (again depending on how we define "local") would be going into 60 to 80 percent of the economy comprised of local business. Somewhere between $34 and $45 trillion would be shifted from global companies to local ones. In fact, a small fraction of short-term banking deposits is being lent to local business, and almost all the $56.5 trillion in long-term investment is going into big business.

What would be the impact if Americans shifted 60 percent of their investment into local businesses? A shift of this magnitude would mean that every community in the United States would have at least $100,000 more capital to invest in local businesses for every resident living in it. If you lived in a small town with 10,000 people, that could mean a billion dollars more of capital to regenerate your economy. If you lived in a small city with 100,000 people, you would have $10 billion more. It is hard to imagine any policy or governmental program that could deliver even a tiny fraction of the potential impact of residents changing their investment choices.

The unequal flow of capital right now is a reminder that the current capital marketplace effectively is a gigantic subsidy for Wall Street. The perceived "competitiveness" of many global businesses has depended on easy money from this tilted investment system. Take that bias away, shrink the available capital, and much of Wall Street crumbles. The activists who pushed to "Occupy Wall Street" should have branded their campaign as "Defund Wall Street."

How did this unequal flow of capital happen in the first place?

How Did Financial Institutions Come to Disfavor Local Business?

Historically, the go-to place for local business in America was the bank. Small banks opened in communities, took in local capital, and lent it back out to residential and commercial customers. Over the past half century, however, there has been a huge consolidation of banks, savings and loans (also called "thrifts"), and even credit unions. Since 1990, the number of FDIC-insured commercial banks has shrunk from 12,343 to 4,630 and FDIC-insured savings institutions from 2,815 to 673.[4] The number of insured credit unions in the United States peaked in the late 1960s at 23,866 and has since shrunk to 5,014.[5] Tens of millions of Americans have had the experience of doing business at a community bank, only to wake up one morning and find that a bigger bank just bought it out.

Why did this happen? Some conservative economists argue that mergers have made banks more efficient. Maybe. But other studies have found that bigger banks actually have higher fees, higher overheads, and more defaults. Mergers are often the result of perverse incentives. The managers of acquiring banks get bonuses for enlarging their institutions, and the shareholders of the acquired bank get a short-term price boost for their stock. It's an unfortunate alliance, because the losers include the long-term shareholders, the customers, and the employees. Meanwhile, antitrust regulators who once policed mergers because of the adverse effects on competition now have effectively fallen asleep at the wheel and, zombie-like, approve almost everything.

After the financial crisis of 2008, Congress passed the Dodd-Frank Act (named after the two key architects, Senator Chris Dodd and Congressman Barney Frank) to tighten regulatory standards on banks, but perversely this has actually accelerated the rate of mergers and acquisitions. Bigger banks absorbed the costs of the new regulations more easily than smaller banks. Congress could have fixed the law by granting exemptions to smaller banks but, instead, in the name of cutting red tape, decided to repeal the whole law. Yes, this might have helped smaller banks' survival a tad, but at the cost of permitting all banks to resume the risky practices that almost blew up the entire financial system.

Here's why consolidation matters. The probability that a dollar deposited in a small bank or credit union will make its way into a small business is three times greater than that of a dollar deposited in a big bank.[6] Even though small- and medium-scale banks represent less than 20 percent of all bank assets, they are responsible for more than half of commercial lending to small business. This explains why one grassroots response to the crisis of 2008 was to launch a campaign called Move Your Money (from global banks to local ones). Local banks, almost by definition, lend almost all their money locally.

But go back to the numbers describing American household financial assets. The securities sector is four times the size of the banking sector. That means that even if Move Your Money had been 100 percent successful, only a small percentage of the financial sector would have been localized.

Why is the securities sector all about big business?

Let's pause for a second and define the term "securities." A security is basically any financial instrument, usually some kind of agreement on paper, that pays a return. It can be a loan paying interest, a stock appreciating, or a royalty payment (usually a percentage of profits or revenue, up to some ceiling). Most securities are regulated by the federal Securities and Exchange Commission (SEC) and its equivalents in every state, which require anyone who issues a security to disclose key facts to purchasers. Where the law gets tricky is that some things that would appear to be securities are exempt. You don't need to register a loan to your spouse or kid, for example. And banks and credit unions are exempt because they are covered by specific banking laws.

But back to our question: How did it become the case that everyone's money is tied up in Wall Street, rather than in the 60–80 percent of the economy made up of local businesses? Why is it that very few local businesses issue securities for grassroots investors?

One explanation is economies of scale. All things being equal, an investment institution prefers big investors in big companies. No matter the size of the company or its long-term profitability, smart investment practice and the law require due diligence before any money changes hands. Say that work costs $100,000 per company. Since your fees will be a percentage of the deal, you'd much rather do the $100,000 of work for Home Depot than Joe's Hardware Store. In fact, when you tell Joe that the work will cost at least $100,000, Joe will likely run out the door cursing and start thinking about early retirement.

Another reason is history. High finance used to be exclusively for a small number of tycoons. Very few Americans, for example, could afford a seat at the New York Stock Exchange. Various reforms pried open finance—stock purchasing now can be done by anyone on E-Trade, for example—but none touched how businesses raise money by issuing securities.

The foundation of US securities law can be found in four pieces of legislation: the Securities Act of 1933, the Exchange Act of 1934, the Investment Advisers Act of 1940, and the Investment Company Act of 1940. Let's focus on the Securities Act. It basically said that every company that wants to sell securities first has to register them with the SEC. The burdens imposed on companies depend a lot on who's buying the securities. If the buyers of the securities are rich people, then the paperwork is pretty light. The law presumes that people with money know what they're doing and, even if they don't, they can afford the loss. But if you want to sell the securities to any average investor, you are required to complete a mountain of legal paperwork and sometimes must get a permission slip from the government first.

In one way, the logic is unassailable. The Securities Act protects Americans from getting swindled and buying swampland in Florida. But the law had another consequence as well, probably unintended. The burden of complying, often $25,000 to $100,000 per securities offering, was reasonable for large companies but not small ones. Local businesses mostly concluded that the legal expenses associated with soliciting nickels and dimes from grassroots investors were not worth it. This explains why most local businesses seeking outside money tend to go to angel investors, venture funds, or other vehicles involving only rich people. The entire investment market thus evolved primarily to serve rich people. Even the first retirement vehicles for the grass roots—the Individual Retirement Account and the 401k—were designed primarily to give wealthy individuals another way to save. It was only later that these were packaged and marketed to grassroots investors.

Securities law calls investors who are rich enough to do what they want "accredited investors." Depending on how you do the math, accredited investors constitute between 1 percent and 5.5 percent of the US population. (See the box.) The rest of the country is "unaccredited"—and that probably means you. Being unaccredited does not mean you can't be an investor. It just means that any loan you give or stock you buy must have the proper legal paperwork done first, before a seller of securities can even talk to you.

The ability of unaccredited investors to buy securities is now changing, thanks in part to the JOBS Act and similar reforms at the state level. Local investment options for unaccredited investors are opening dramatically. But because the marketplace is immature, you can't depend on investment professionals to find good investments, evaluate them, and create a portfolio of them. That falls to you.

Are You Accredited?

The SEC offers three different ways an investor can be deemed accredited. An investor must earn $200,000 per year individually or $300,000 per year as a couple or have a household with $1 million of wealth (excluding the value of the house). A business is deemed accredited if it has assets over $5 million. How many Americans are actually accredited?

On the first two criteria, data from the IRS are helpful. In 2016, the most recent year for which data are available, the total number of tax filings above $200,000 (adjusted gross income) was 6,900,372. According to the US Census, the population in 2016 was about 323 million. Even assuming that every tax filer above $200,000 was single, accredited investors would constitute 2.1 percent of the population. In fact, however, the number of taxpayers filing as a couple was 5,893,163—about 85 percent of the total—and these taxpayers would be subjected to the higher threshold of $300,000. Because the IRS data are presented in a large bracket of $200,000 to $500,000, we can only guess how many are accredited couples. But a fair assessment would say that, by income, 1–2 percent of the population is accredited.

On the third criterion of wealth, the website *DQYDJ .com*, which specializes in providing financial data, suggests that $1 million in wealth, excluding your home, puts you in the 91st percentile of American households. Since there are about 125 million American households, the site argues that 12,417,040 are "accredited investor households." The number of accredited investors would include the head of the household plus the spouse. According to the 2010 Census, 48 percent of the households have a spouse. This would suggest about 18 million accredited investors, or about 5.5 percent of the population.

The percentage of the population that is accredited has gone up over time with inflation, rising incomes, and rising stock portfolios. Many at the SEC, however, would like to tighten the admission standards and make the accredited investor club more exclusive.

The Bottom Line

Most of the US economy—by jobs and output—can be found in locally owned enterprises. The evidence suggests that, on balance, these companies are at least as profitable as their global counterparts. And while all businesses are risky, there is no good evidence that local businesses are riskier than their global counterparts, at least if you focus on existing local businesses rather than startups. Some features of local businesses pose special risk, but other features make them less risky. A smart local investor must weigh all these factors.

Perhaps the biggest risk facing a local investor is the immaturity of the existing marketplace. But because of the peculiar evolution of banking and securities law, nearly all our investment dollars are flowing into global business, and that's where most finance professionals are focused as well. This means, for the moment, you need to invest serious time to find local businesses, evaluate them, manage your investments, and create your own local portfolio. It's satisfying work, however, when you weigh the ways in which these investments boost your community.

4

BEATING THE STREET

The first rule of smart investing is this: *Be skeptical, very skeptical.* Almost everyone who calls themselves a financial expert has strong opinions about the great rates of return you can expect from their pet recommendations. My advice is to discount or ignore all of them—including mine. Again, my mission is not to help you get rich quick, but rather to widen your universe of promising investment alternatives to consider. I would like you to start thinking about a dozen strategies that can put your money to work locally. Many of these strategies—if you're smart about it—will generate returns that match or beat Wall Street.

Wall Street has assumed an almost mythical status as a place where fortunes are made and lost overnight and where the machinations of the global economic system are set. It also refers to the home of one of the most important financial institutions in the world, the New York Stock Exchange. Fairly or not, the performance of the stock market is the gold standard against which you and everyone else will weigh your investment choices. So let's understand exactly what that benchmark is.

What's the Likely Return from the Stock Market?

If you read columns by financial advisors or listen to their radio shows or podcasts, you will find no shortage of bullish prognosticators who will tell you that if you patiently leave your money in the stock market for many years, you can expect a rate of return of 10, 12, even 18 percent. (See the box.) My judgment is that these numbers are wildly inflated.

Inflated Claims by Investment "Experts"

"Like nearly any fund, an S&P 500 index fund offers immediate diversification, allowing you to own a piece of all of those companies. . . . Over time, the index has returned about 10 percent annually."

—*James Royal, "Best Investments for 2019," on Bankrate.com*[1]

"According to historical records, the average annual return [of the S&P 500] since its inception in 1926 through 2018 is approximately 10%."

—*Investopedia*[2]

"The current average annual return from 1923 (the year of the S&P's inception) through 2016 is 12.25%."

—*Dave Ramsey*[3]

"Barring a dramatic, unforeseen event like the 1987 stock market crash, the S&P 500 will have posted an average return of nearly 18%, *each year,* over the past decade, according to S&P Dow Jones Indices. . . . Kicking yourself for not buying?"

—*Money Magazine, 2019*[4]

"Attention investors: Not earning a consistent 18% to 21%? Then you're losing big time!"

—*Radio ad for National Reality Investment Advisors, 2019*

A better place to understand the performance of the marketplace is in the work of Professor Robert J. Shiller, a Yale University professor of economics and winner of the 2013 Nobel Prize in Economics.[5] He's also cocreator of the Case-Shiller housing index, and he has spent much of his professional life mining data to deflate hyperbolic claims from the financial industry. His bestseller, published eight years before the financial meltdown of 2008, was presciently titled *Irrational Exuberance.* On Shiller's website, you can find the historical performance of the Standard & Poor's index every month since it was started in 1926. He also uses other available data to extrapolate performance of the stock market, month by month, since 1871. He provides data on inflation, prices, and dividends. If you adjust for inflation and add dividends, the average rate of return on the stock market in any given twelve-month period, from 1871 to the present, is about 8 percent.[6]

Bulls are convinced that technology, ingenuity, and American entrepreneurial energy will push this number higher. Why should the past dictate the future? A new era of turbo-charged capitalism lies ahead, spurred by the entry of billions of new people into the global marketplace. Just look at the spectacular performance of the stock market since 2008.

To which the bears say, "Bull!" The future could be quite grim, with a climate catastrophe, new pandemics, food and water shortages, and so forth. Shiller himself said recently, "We're launching a trade war. Aren't people thinking about that? Is that a good thing? I don't know, but I'm thinking it's likely to be bad times in the stock market."[7]

Personally, I'm with the bears, but not because I'm an alarmist. It's because the 8 percent return implicit in Shiller's data must be understood with a bunch of footnotes. For most investors, there's a transaction cost of 1 percent or so per year associated with buying, trading, and managing the securities (if you haven't done so, please read the fine print in your mutual fund annual reports). A lot of the gains in Wall Street's early years also reflected most large companies paying dividends of 5 percent or so per year. Today, most large companies do not pay dividends at all, and if they do, they are significantly smaller. And we are currently in the midst of all-time stock market highs—the average annual return since 2010 has been over 12 percent—which suggests that a serious correction is overdue. The average annual return since 2000, during which we've seen at least two such corrections, was a paltry 4.7 percent.

Also consider this: The 8 percent number reflects a perfect stock portfolio, left in perfect index funds, for the perfect long term where no timing mistakes are made. None of us, sadly, are perfect; and we enter and exit the market at moments dictated by our beautifully imperfect lives.

Finally, consider that most of us invest in the stock market by picking stocks or investing in several "expertly" assembled portfolios available through our mutual fund or retirement fund. The vast majority of these funds *underperform* the market in any given year; over five or ten years, nearly all of them do.[8] If most professional fund managers underperform the stock market averages, so will you.

Also, let's question the premise that the stock market is the right benchmark for success. Because the stock market is so risky, even for long-term investors, many of us also choose to invest in more reliable financial instruments, such as bank CDs, money market accounts, US savings bonds, and currencies. These typically generate returns more in the range of 1–3 percent.

For the purposes of the rest of this chapter, I'm going to assume that to match or beat the global markets, a local investor will want to generate a healthy return of at least 5 percent per year.[9] By comparing local investments with high-risk stock investments rather than low-risk investments like bonds, money market accounts, CDs, and so forth, I am creating a very demanding goal for the strategies I'm proposing.

You might decide you are slightly more bullish or bearish, but the important point is this: Having a baseline of comparison of 5 percent, give or take, leads to dramatically different expectations and decisions than having a phantasmagorical baseline of 10 percent. It opens up all kinds of local investment opportunities you otherwise would have overlooked.

Drum roll. I now would like you to consider twelve ways you can invest locally, most of which can beat Wall Street.

Strategy 1: Invest in Yourself by Paying Off Credit Cards

As my own tragic story in Chapter 1 underscored, investing in yourself is an important form of local investment. From a community economy perspective, credit cards are public enemy number one. Not only do they addict many of us, crack-like, to purchasing what we cannot afford, but they also cause major leaks to your local economy. A 2 to 3 percent fee that goes to the home office of Visa, Mastercard, Discover, or American Express drains away revenues from your local businesses, which cover their costs by raising their prices. Even worse is the interest, currently *averaging* over 17 percent, which means millions of Americans are paying a usurious 25–30 percent in interest each year.[10] Overall, Americans owe nearly a trillion dollars of credit card debt, and card holders average a balance of over $6,300.[11]

If you are currently paying 20 percent on a credit card, every dollar you deploy to reduce your credit card debt, instead of investing in the stock market, will generate a net return of 15 percent per year. (That is, 20 percent not paid, minus the 5 percent return forgone from Wall Street.) The logical imperative is clear: None of us should be putting a penny into conventional stocks and bonds until we are 100 percent free of credit card debt.

If you can't resist the perks of a credit card—maybe you want airline miles associated with certain cards—fine. Keep the card but be absolutely sure to pay off your balance 100 percent each month. Avoid credit card debt like the Ebola virus.

My recommendation is to open an account at a local bank or credit union and pay all your bills with a debit card. This way, your money stays local, the fees recirculate within your community, and you save yourself from onerous interest charges and penalties.

Skeptics will insist that this advice—along with several of the items that follow—is not about investment at all, but rather personal financial management. Nonsense. This is a distinction without a difference, and ignoring it is one of the conceptual shifts essential to becoming a successful local investor. Yes, in a perfect world, we all would run perfectly efficient lives, with ourselves and our children being debt free, with all of us owning our homes free and clear, and with significant savings that we then can invest in other businesses. Except for a small percentage of the American public, this is a unicorn planet that does not exist. A recent analysis by the Federal Reserve found that nearly 40 percent of us do not have enough spare cash to cover an unexpected $400 emergency.[12] About a third of US households do not own their homes, and many of the rest are still paying mortgages.

Don't pay attention to the industry's absurd silos. The money is all coming from the same place—your pocket. When you have maximized your personal—and local—returns from the first items on this list, then, and only then, should you consider investing in other people, projects, and businesses.

Strategy 2: Invest in Your Kids' Future

Cutting up your kids' credit cards is really part of option number one, but I'm listing it separately to make a point that applies to many of the other strategies that follow. What's good for the goose is good for the gander and all the other people who flock around you.

If your daughter has racked up an unsustainable credit card debt of $20,000, make her a deal: I'll buy out your credit card and pay it off, and you can pay me the $20,000 at an interest rate of 5 percent per year. You get a great new income source, and your daughter gets a new lease on life. (You might promise to post on her social media accounts the most embarrassing pictures of her childhood if she ever opens another credit card again or falls short on a payment.)

Remember the tale of my own foolish financial choices I described in Chapter 1? Remember that $80,000 debt to the IRS that I partially paid on my credit cards? The way I got myself out of my new credit card debt was to convince a half-dozen dear friends to lend me money so I could pay off the cards. (They were the people to whom I dedicated this book.) I'm now paying them back over five years at 5 percent (though one friend refused to accept interest payments). They are doing as well as they would have on Wall Street, and I was able to get back on my feet financially.

The first person I approached with this proposal was Cathy Berry of Vermont, who had been an important supporter of various local economy initiatives. Before the ask, I was absolutely terrified. I feared that sharing my financial challenges might poison my relationship with her and that she would lecture me with some version of Ben Franklin's admonition: "Lend money . . . to a friend and thou will lose him." She agreed to my request to set up a telephone call. We spoke for almost two hours. I was stunned to discover that she actually had been thinking about investment opportunities like this herself. She thanked me for stepping forward, sharing my story, making myself vulnerable, and allowing us together—not just her—to prove how this type of investment could succeed. Reflecting on our relationships (the payback is almost complete), she recently wrote, "We need to inspire others to help someone because they are doing the right thing. If we support the common good, we improve everyone's life."

Why stop at credit cards? If your daughter has a student loan for 7 percent, pay it off immediately and have her pay the amount back to you at 5 percent. An estimated 44 million young Americans, including two-thirds of all recent college graduates, have $1.5 trillion of student debt.[13] More than 12 million have debt between $10,000 and $25,000, 2.5 million have debt over $100,000, and 610,000 have debt over $200,000. They are typically paying interest rates between 5 and 7.6 percent, though millions are in default and paying more.[14] This is a huge opportunity to make money and keep thousands of your kids' dollars out of Wall Street.

Strategy 3: Invest in a Home

For most Americans, the only significant wealth they will enjoy in their retirement will be held in the equity of their homes. Therefore, even though the single largest expenditure the typical family makes every year is for housing, this choice is inherently about investment, not just spending.

And getting it right is essential not only for personal prosperity but also for your community's well-being. As long as Uncle Sam continues to provide tax deductions for interest paid on the mortgage of your primary residence—one of the biggest subsidies the federal government offers—"right" means becoming a homeowner. In most foreseeable scenarios, investing in your own house pays better than Wall Street.

Let's perform a thought experiment: Suppose you have $50,000 in savings, and you're wondering whether to invest it in Wall Street. You also are very disciplined with your own personal spending and have decided that you have $1,073 to spend each month on your housing. You can put $50,000 in Wall Street and rent a place to live, or you can use that money as a 20 percent down payment on a $250,000 home with a thirty-year mortgage. Put simply, you can pay $1,073 in monthly rent and be a stock market mini-tycoon or pay just $1,073 in monthly mortgage, acquire a home, and skip the stock market. Which should you do?

To run the numbers, we need to make a few simplifying assumptions. Let's assume you find an interest rate of 5 percent for your mortgage. (As of this writing, you can get closer to 4 percent with a strong credit rating.) To make the case for being a stock-market tycoon especially strong, let's also assume that over thirty years your property does not appreciate a penny. And finally let's assume, as discussed earlier in this chapter, that Wall Street delivers a steady 5 percent return each year on your investment.

Chart 1 shows what happens over thirty years. Under the scenario where you remain a renter and invest in Wall Street, your $50,000 investment grows impressively to $166,000. When you cash out in year thirty, however, you will then need to pay taxes. If your marginal tax rate is 20 percent, you have really netted about $133,000. Put another way, taxes reduce your annual Wall Street return from 5 percent to 3.3 percent, which is an inconvenient fact most of us forget.

Chart 1. Wall Street vs. Owning a Home over Thirty Years (base case)

	MORTGAGE	RENT
Monthly Housing Payment	($1,073)	($1,073)
Wall Street Investment	$0	($50,000)
Down Payment	($50,000)	$0
Return from Wall Street (5%)	$0	$216,097
House Principal Payments	($200,000)	$0
House Interest Payments	($186,512)	$0
Rent Avoided	$386,280	$0
House Value after 30 Years	$250,000	$0
Pre-Tax Gain	$199,768	$166,097
Tax Reduction (20% for Mortgage Interest)	$37,302	$0
Tax on House Gains	$0	$0
Tax on Wall Street Gains (20%)	$0	($33,219)
Post-Tax Gain	$237,070	$132,878
Asset Growth over 30 Years	4.74x	2.66x
Annual Growth Rate	5.32%	3.31%

If you invest the same $50,000 in your own mortgage for thirty years, the most important gain is that you avoid $386,000 of rent. Rather than enriching a landlord each month, you are growing your own personal wealth. In all, your avoided rent is more than double the interest you would pay on your mortgage ($186,000). Plus, you get an income tax deduction for the interest you paid on the mortgage. If you sold the house after year thirty, moreover, you would not need to pay taxes on up to $250,000 of gains—but, again, we are assuming zero appreciation of your house. Even with that very demanding assumption, your bottom-line gain would be $237,000—or an annual return of about 5.3 percent, which beats what you would have earned from Wall Street.

There are, of course, ways of manipulating the assumptions so that being a renter and investing in Wall Street makes more sense. If your house loses value over thirty years—perhaps a toxic waste dump is suddenly discovered in the backyard—you'll be better off renting. If you live in a locality that taxes property heavily, you might prefer the stock market—though you'll pay those taxes anyway in the form of less house for your rental dollar. Or if interest rates suddenly spike into the double digits, perhaps because the federal deficit has triggered the double-digit level of inflation seen in the 1970s, it might make sense to avoid buying a house. But most of us assume, quite reasonably, that our houses will gain value, which makes the case for investing in your own home stronger.

Some will counter that not every American can afford a home. Unless your credit rating is defective, however, this statement is misleading. Not every American can afford a split-level with four bedrooms and an acre of lawn. If you have more limited means, the goal is to find a more modest property that fits your financial profile. You might look for a small unit in a co-op apartment, a cohousing community, or a land trust. Only if you have no savings for a down payment is becoming a homeowner difficult (though not impossible), but in that case you would not have funds to invest in Wall Street anyway.

If you decide to become a homeowner, you also can increase your social rate of return further by getting your mortgage at a community bank or credit union rather than a banking behemoth. Keeping your interest payments local enables your bank to make more loans to local business. Many banks, even local ones, short-circuit the multiplier effect by reselling the loans to big banks. As you shop around for a mortgage, one of your questions should be whether yours will be sold on the secondary market. If the answer is "no," you can be sure your interest payments are recycling back into your community.

Strategy 4: Invest in Paying Down Your Mortgage Faster

Suppose you already have a mortgage, you have no credit card debt, and you have extra money to invest. Might it make sense to invest *those* dollars in Wall Street? Probably not. Because under most reasonable assumptions, you will get a higher return if you use that money to pay down your mortgage more quickly. Again, the tax advantages of your home, even with a smaller mortgage, will beat your long-term gains from Wall Street.

Let's build on the previous example and maintain all its assumptions except one. This time let's assume you have

$100,000 to invest in the house instead of $50,000. If you become a homeowner, place $100,000 down (40 percent of the value), and maintain the same mortgage payment of $1,073 per month, you will be able to pay off the property in seventeen and a half years instead of thirty. The alternative is to rent and put $100,000 into Wall Street instead of $50,000.

Chart 2 shows what happens. This time, your thirty-year gain of 4 percent as a homeowner still beats your Wall Street gain of 3.3 percent. Notice that as a Wall Street investor, your rate of return stays constant, because we assume the annual return on stocks (5 percent) and your marginal tax rate (20 percent) stay the same. As a homeowner, your rate of return declines slightly as you borrow less from the bank, because you are losing the tax advantages from the mortgage interest deduction. But in this example, you still do better than Wall Street.

If you continue down this road and pay more and more up front, the tax advantages of the mortgage interest deduction ultimately disappear, and then the Wall Street investment finally looks more attractive. But remember why: *We assumed that your house would gain no value over thirty years.* So, sure, buying a house outright that you know won't appreciate and denying yourself federal tax deductions, rather than putting your money into a stock market appreciating 5 percent per year, is not a great investment strategy.

The more realistic assumption is that your house *will* appreciate. Robert Shiller suggests that historically the real estate market gains about 2 percent per year above inflation.[15] If that holds true, paying off your mortgage more quickly will almost always be a better bet than Wall Street.

Chart 2. Wall Street vs. Owning a Home over Thirty Years (paying mortgage faster)

	MORTGAGE	RENT
Monthly Housing Payment	($1,073)	($1,073)
Wall Street Investment	$0	($100,000)
Down Payment	($100,000)	$0
Return from Wall Street (5%)	$0	$432,194
House Principal Payments	($150,000)	$0
House Interest Payments	($75,369)	$0
Rent Avoided	$386,280	$0
House Value after 30 Years	$250,000	$0
Pre-Tax Gain	$310,911	$332,194
Tax Reduction (20% for Mortgage Interest)	$15,074	$0
Tax on House Gains	$0	$0
Tax on Wall Street Gains (20%)	$0	($66,439)
Post-Tax Gain	$325,985	$265,755
Asset Growth over 30 Years	3.26x	2.66x
Annual Growth Rate	4.02%	3.31%

Focusing your investment on a home rather than Wall Street confers another advantage. For Wall Street investments, you are relying on boardroom decisions and market circumstances over which you have no control. For your home investment, you are the captain of your own ship. You can decide to keep the paint shiny, the lawn mowed, and the roof repaired. And if you are really ambitious, you can help your neighbors maximize their home values by running a top-notch neighborhood association or serving on the school board. Investing in your own home effectively means running your own hedge fund.

Strategy 5: Invest in Cutting Your Daily Bills

If you look at your family's expenditures beyond housing, you will see plenty of other opportunities for local investment. Consider your utility bill. According to the 2016 annual Consumer Expenditure Survey, the typical "consumer unit" (which means, roughly, a family) spends $3,884 per year on utilities, which include electricity, gas, sewage, and garbage pickup. Can you get a higher rate of return through the purchase of efficiency measures and renewable energy devices than you would by investing conventionally on Wall Street? Absolutely.

To answer this question, let's introduce another term that economists use called a "wasting asset," which refers to an asset that depreciates over time. If you install $1,000 worth of energy-efficiency measures, it may or may not increase the value of your house by $1,000. And the longer you wait until resale, the less likely your investment will have any influence on the house price at all. For assets like these, you want to pay more attention to your immediate savings. Some consumers look for their investments to pay back quickly, in perhaps three to five years. Others might be comfortable with a twenty-year payback. You should ask yourself what payback period you yourself are comfortable with. (See the box.)

How to Think about Your Own Payback

If you want to get serious about investing in your life, one question you will have to answer concerns your expected rate of return for investments in wasting assets—that is, assets that won't be around forever. Most of us are wildly inconsistent in our thinking.

When we are thinking about investing in a major upgrade in our home's energy efficiency, perhaps by replacing our drafty windows or improving the insulation in our walls and ceilings, we often insist on a three-year "payback." In other words, we want to earn back everything we paid for the retrofit within three years.

Yet for other things in life, we use broader time horizons. For our homes, we embrace mortgages that are thirty to forty years. For student loans, we might choose loans for ten to twenty years. For cars, financing arrangements might be for five to ten years.

When larger institutions think about paybacks, they often assume decades for the payback. When a law firm purchases a building, it might want its costs (relative to renting) to be paid back in twenty years. When a utility purchases a power plant, it could be looking at thirty years. When your government wants to pay for a bridge, it might float bonds for fifty years.

People and institutions, of course, are entitled to think differently. I encourage you to pick a number that works for you and apply it consistently.

You might ask yourself how long your asset will last. If your new, highly efficient HVAC unit is expected to last for seven years, give yourself seven years for the payback. But what about insulation in your home? It will produce benefits as long as your home is standing, which could be a hundred years. In that case think about how long you expect to stay in your home. If you anticipate staying there for another ten years, until the kids go off to college, then your payback period should be ten years.

For the purposes of this section, let's assume you are comfortable with a ten-year payback. What would you earn if you invest $1,000 in Wall Street for ten years? At a 5 percent rate of return per year, at the end of year ten, your investment will be worth $1,629. For a wasting asset to deliver an equivalent return over ten years, it will need to pay you $162.90 per year over ten years (that is, $1,629 divided by ten). You will therefore want a 16.29 percent annual return on your investment for ten years.

So, can a $1,000 investment in energy efficiency save you $163 per year? The answer depends on where you live, what kind of efficiency measures you've installed already, what the price of energy is locally, and so forth. But generally speaking, this level of savings should not be difficult to attain. The American Council for an Energy-Efficient Economy argues that "light" improvements in a home's energy efficiency can deliver a "whopping 18.5% return annually."[16] McKinsey & Company, the nation's preeminent consulting firm, agrees, estimating in 2008 that $170 billion of energy-efficiency investments are possible worldwide by 2020, which could generate an internal rate of return of at least 10 percent.[17] The *average* rate of return of all these investments, McKinsey suggests, would be 17 percent.

Here are some specific examples: An investment of $625 to replace a pre-1980 toilet with a water-efficient WaterSense will save $100 per year in water costs—a 16 percent rate of return.[18] With a budget of up to $400, replacing your home's most frequently used light fixtures or bulbs with Energy Star models can save you $75 per year—an 18.5 percent return per year.[19] If your fixtures can use LED bulbs or you install the appliances yourself, you can generate a higher rate of return. A $350 programmable thermostat in your home could save you $84 per year—a 24 percent annual return.[20] Spending $500 to add more insulation and air seal your home could save you $168 in annual heating and cooling costs—a 34 percent annual return.[21]

If we relax our payback assumption even slightly, the opportunities grow exponentially. For example, installation of solar electric systems on your roof, after you take full advantage of tax credits and resale opportunities for surplus electricity, will deliver nearly a 14 percent per year return.[22] If you give yourself a payback period of fifteen years instead of ten, you then beat Wall Street. If the price of solar panels continues to drop, as it has over the past decade, solar investments might hit this milestone by the time this book reaches its second or third printing.

Another assumption we might relax is that energy-efficiency measures do not raise the value of a house. According to a study by Build It Green, a nonprofit based in Oakland, California, homes in Los Angeles County with energy-efficiency upgrades saw a 6 percent increase in value in 2014.[23] For investments that will last as long as the house, such as insulation and high-efficiency windows, it's easy to see how home buyers will pay attention. Even new household appliances, with a shorter lifetime, can impress buyers.

There's no reason to limit this logic just to energy. You could imagine all kinds of investments that effectively could pay for themselves over ten years:

- An investment of $1,000 in a greenhouse could easily save you more than $163 in annual spending on fruits and vegetables.

- An investment of $1,000 in a high-quality bicycle could save you more than $163 in annual gasoline expenditures (in fact, if you loved biking, this number could be your monthly savings).

- An investment of $1,000 in a top-of-the-line espresso machine, if it prevents you from buying one Starbucks grande latte per week, would significantly exceed the targeted 16 percent rate of return.

- An investment of $1,000 in an exercise machine, if it led to at least one or two days of work not missed or an avoided visit to your doctor, would be better than Wall Street.

- An investment of $10,000 in your own education would make sense if it increased your salary by at least $1,629 per year.

All these investments require more than writing a check—they require changes in your behavior and, in some cases, changes in your lifestyle. But if you're someone who thinks personal-growth activities are valuable and fun to do anyway, why not prioritize these investments over Wall Street, enjoy the extra cash, and live longer?

Strategy 6: Invest in Your Co-op

For many years, consumer cooperatives presented one of the few ways the grass roots could invest locally. The reason was that co-op memberships were not considered securities, which meant that a group of well-organized grassroots folks could set up and run a co-op with very little legal cost.

Common consumer cooperatives include credit unions, electric utility co-ops, and grocery co-ops, but you can find examples for almost every good and service, from recreational equipment (Recreational Equipment Inc.) to burial services (the Co-op Funeral Home of People's Memorial). A survey of the US cooperative landscape by a group of scholars at the University of Wisconsin found nearly 30,000 cooperatives operating at 73,000 locations.[24] The vast majority are consumer cooperatives, with 343 million memberships (many people belong to multiple co-ops, hence the number of memberships exceeds the US population). The cooperative sector owns $3 trillion in assets, generates half a trillion dollars a year in revenue, and pays 856,000 people $25 billion in annual wages. Significantly, almost all cooperatives are locally owned businesses.

Co-ops differ from corporations in several important ways. While both have boards that oversee management, corporate boards are elected by shareholders who generally cast one vote for each share of stock they own. Co-ops, in contrast, allocate one vote per member, independent of how much money they put into the enterprise. Co-op members believe this is a more democratic framework for running a business.

While corporations allocate profits based on shares—the more shares you own, the more dividends you collect and the more appreciation you enjoy—co-ops allocate returns based on your contribution during the previous year. Those returns are called patronage payments. The more you shop at a grocery co-op, for example, the higher your annual patronage payment.

Co-op members usually don't think of themselves as investors, but they are. Consider the Central Co-op in Seattle, a grocery business with 14,600 members who each paid $100 to join. In 2015, sales exceeded $24 million, and $124,610 was distributed to member-owners through patronage payments. As a matter of investment, $124,610 split over 14,600 members is $8.54 per member or an 8.5 percent annual return on a $100 membership—significantly better than the 5 percent members would get on Wall Street. That's the *average* return. Co-op members who shopped more than the average member earned higher returns.

Co-ops also turn to their members for capital projects. When Weaver Street Market in Research Triangle, North Carolina, wanted to build a third store for its rapidly expanding membership, it needed $1 million in new capital. Weaver Street decided to borrow the money from its members paying 5–7 percent per year, depending on how long they were willing to invest. These kinds of deals regularly pop up everywhere.

Some co-ops go further and use their members' capital to invest in other businesses. Co-op Power in Western Massachusetts uses some of its members' initial fees to invest in local energy companies—providing biofuels, firewood, solar panels, efficiency audits, etc.—and then members get discounted access to their products. The NorthEast Investment Co-op in Minneapolis and the NYC Real Estate Investment Cooperative use members' capital to invest in affordable housing projects. Poudre Valley Community Farms in Colorado is a multistakeholder cooperative that invites both consumer and farmer members to invest in the purchase of farmland and rewards them in food discounts and patronage payments.

Strategy 7: Invest in Your Favorite Local Business

Even before the emergence of investment crowdfunding, most communities had a few exceptional businesses that raised capital locally. Consider Quimper Mercantile in Port Townsend, Washington, a town of 10,000 north of Seattle. In recent years, Port Townsend had seen its premiere variety stores—JCPenney and Sprouse-Reitz—move out or shut down. Residents complained that they had nowhere to buy socks or underwear. The best you could do was drive an hour to shopping malls. The mayor, Michelle Sandoval, called a meeting when Swain's Outdoors shut down. As she told *Seattle Business*, "A real town needs a real store."

Thanks to local investors, Port Townsend established the Quimper Mercantile in a refurbished 16,000-square-foot space that Swain's once occupied. Essential to the success of this endeavor was local stock issued through a direct public offering (DPO), which means the company sold shares directly to the public. (See the adjacent box for a short overview of securities law.)

A Short Primer on Exemptions from Securities Filings

If you're a business and you want to take a one-dollar loan from a single unaccredited investor, you will have to prepare a private placement memorandum and other legal disclosures for federal and state securities regulators that could easily cost you $15,000 or more. And if you want your securities to be publicly bought, sold, and traded on the New York Stock Exchange, expect legal costs starting at hundreds of thousands of dollars per year. That's why businesses seek to fit within an "exemption" to full-blown federal and state registrations. In the arcane world of securities law, an exemption does not mean you're excused from all legal work, just that the burden is lighter.

Here's a quick list of the common exemptions businesses use if they want to sell securities to unaccredited investors:

- *Regulation D*[25]—A business can sell an unlimited amount of securities to an unlimited number of accredited investors and no more than thirty-five unaccredited investors. It cannot advertise, however, which means it's mostly limited to the famous three Fs—friends, family, and fools. It must provide unaccredited investors with legal documents that contain the same information as required in a registration.

- *Regulation A*[26]—Under Tier 1 of "Reg A," a business can sell up to $20 million of securities within a year to an unlimited number of accredited and unaccredited investors. The disclosure documents, while less demanding than a full-blown registration, can easily cost $50–100,000. Permission also must be sought from every state where securities are sold. The JOBS Act enacted a Tier 2 for offerings up to $50 million, and these securities can be sold nationwide without state-by-state approvals.

- *Intrastate Offering Exemption*[27]—A business can sell securities to an unlimited number of investors, including unaccredited investors, in a single state—and only in that state. Some states are draconian in the legal work they require, while others are permissive. Most states set a modest upper limit on your offering. The intrastate offering exemption is designed to connect small businesses with local investors. Because these offerings sell securities directly to grassroots investors, rather than through underwriters, they are called direct public offerings (DPOs).

- *Crowdfunding*—See the box, "Four Flavors of Crowdfunding," in the Introduction.

Peter Quinn is the cofounder of the Mercantile and serves as its CEO. He is also the executive director of the Economic Development Council (EDC) of Jefferson County, which goes by the name "Team Jefferson." After efforts to get an existing business to take over Swain's space failed, Quinn and his partners decided to restart the business on their own. Using a direct public offering, Quimper raised over $700,000 from local resident investors and opened its doors on October 11, 2012.

The store, Quinn said, "provides everyday things so people don't have to drive 40 minutes to get what they need. We'll probably do $2.7 million in sales in 2019. We will be profitable for the sixth year in a row. We sold shares of $100 apiece. People of all capabilities purchased the shares. We have 830 shareholders and they are some of our best customers." So far, no dividends have been paid out, because "maintaining the vibrancy of local shopping options, accumulating 60 days of operating reserves, and eliminating debt are more important to investors than profit." The company is also seeking to strengthen employees' pay and benefits. Quimper added four new staff in 2019, bringing the total workforce to fifteen. They each earn an average of $26 per hour and receive twenty-five days per year of sick or personal leave. The board hopes to pay out dividends after eliminating the debt by 2021.

Putting together a public offering, Quinn argues, was challenging but doable. "We had to go through an attorney review, but we didn't have $100,000 to spend." So, the team wrote the eighty-page legal document themselves. They had to go through three rounds before the final documents were approved by state securities regulators, but by doing most of the work themselves, they kept attorney fees down to around $2,000.

The biggest challenge in writing the prospectus and getting it approved by the state was to accurately portray the risk. "Doing a DPO for a pure startup was very risky," explains

Quinn. "People giving us $700,000 didn't know if we would make it happen or not. State regulators wanted to make sure that we gave an accurate picture that people might not get their money back."

Other businesses with deeply loyal consumers— bookstores, breweries, donut shops, restaurants—have done DPOs as well to raise capital from their fans. To be able to raise funds from grassroots investors, all these companies had to register their securities with federal and state authorities. Again, full-blown registrations are very expensive, so most of these companies pursued what's called an "exemption." In the world of securities law, an exemption does not mean you don't have to make any filings with federal and state authorities, only that the filings are less burdensome.

When "two real guys" in Vermont, also known as Ben and Jerry, needed capital to grow their ice cream company, they did what was called an "intrastate offering." This has always been available in all fifty states and allows a company to raise capital just from residents within the state. Those co-op investment opportunities we talked about earlier, for example, were usually intrastate offerings.

The emergence of investment crowdfunding has increased the number and variety of businesses in which you can invest. "Crowdfunding" means that funds come from many small contributors and in many flavors. Thanks to the JOBS Act, any company can now raise up to $1,070,000 relatively easily from any investor. Even the poorest unaccredited investor is now allowed to invest up to $2,200 per year, and those with incomes above $107,000 can invest more. A company interested in crowdfunding must place its offering on a federally licensed portal, such as Wefunder or Honeycomb Credit, of which there are now about three dozen. They typically charge businesses a small amount of money up front and a fee of 5–8 percent on the total raise if it's successful.

One tricky thing about investment crowdfunding is that the federally licensed portals must, by law, allow any US investor to invest in any company, which means that a lot of the crowdfunding is not local. You will need to shop around on each portal to find companies in or near your community. Some of the national portals, however, are contemplating creating local marketplaces to help businesses and investors in the same region find one another. In the meantime, you can discover which companies in your state are crowdfunding through the site Investibule (*www.investibule.co*).

Another place where you will find local investment opportunities in businesses is inside your state. Remember that more than two-thirds of the states also have passed crowdfunding laws, and a few permit intrastate portals selling securities. An example is Milk Money, based in Burlington, Vermont. As soon as a site like this opens up in your state, check it regularly for local investment opportunities.

It's too early to tell how many of these investments will exceed the 5 percent return you would get on Wall Street. If you shop around, you probably can find companies taking loans that pay annual interest of 5 percent or more. If you are buying stock, you will want to find companies that aspire to pay dividends of 5 percent. True, your stock might appreciate. But until there is a designed marketplace for buying, selling, and exchanging local stock—effectively a local stock exchange—you may find it very difficult to monetize your gains from even a highly successful local business.

Strategy 8: Invest in Your Favorite Nonprofit or Place of Worship

Don't forget that businesses include nonprofits. Bellwether Housing, a nonprofit based in Seattle, recently made a crowdfunding offering to help its campaign build 750 new affordable apartments in a region known for skyrocketing property values and growing legions of homeless people. Its Wefunder listing says, "These 750 homes will support an estimated 2,400 residents: preschool teachers, students, retirees, bartenders, small business owners, musicians, orderlies, and young children. Every home will be near public transit, with access to jobs, schools and community resources. It's better for families, our community, and the environment when people can afford to live near where they work."

Bellwether had already lined up substantial funding for this project from banks, social impact investors, and various governmental agencies, so the crowdfunding ask really just filled a modest gap. Every grassroots dollar invested effectively unlocks $29 in capital from these sources. Investors receive a promissory note paying 2 percent per year, with quarterly payments.

Investing in a nonprofit might sound odd, since nonprofits by definition cannot issue stock or ownership shares. A nonprofit, however, has to operate as a business, at least in some respects. It needs a bank account, invests assets or spare cash it has, and even launches capital projects every now and then. Significantly, it can borrow.

A nonprofit seeking capital needs to follow the same securities rules that other businesses do, which effectively means choosing the right "exemption" to a securities registration and then doing all the necessary legal paperwork. Some states, however, make it relatively easy for nonprofits to issue securities through their intrastate offerings.

Here's a suggestion: If you're on the board of an organization that's leasing space—maybe a fraternal organization like the Elks, or a labor union, or even a church—encourage your board colleagues to consider real-estate ownership by borrowing from your members. Which leads naturally to your ninth option.

Strategy 9: Invest in Local Real Estate

One surprise from the short history of legalized federal crowdfunding is that a growing number of investors are shifting their investments from businesses to land, buildings, and housing. This reflects perhaps a preference for investing, not in a dream, but in something tangible like a house, an apartment building, or a shopping center. It also reflects a perception about risk. While many businesses, especially startups, can go completely out of business and lose all their investors' capital, few real estate ventures will lose all their value. Many real estate projects also combine a diverse assortment of properties and units, and this diversification further brings down risk.

Before the JOBS Act was passed in 2012, land investing primarily occurred through personal, family, and partnership purchases and through real estate investment trusts (REITs). Participants typically were accredited investors only. But crowdfunding has opened up this universe to grassroots investors.

The first crowdfunding site to offer real estate investment opportunities was Fundrise, started by Ben and Dan Miller, two brothers who have long been part of a successful developer family in Washington, DC. Initially, they offered properties online to accredited investors, but now anyone can invest in their portfolios. Between 2014 and 2018, investors placing as little as $500 into a pool of properties now worth more than $1 billion have earned an annual rate of return between 8.5 percent and 12.5 percent. The pools offered are not geographically focused, but that could change.

Meanwhile, there are crowdfunding portals with community-specific real estate deals. Small Change, for example, is currently offering grassroots investors the opportunity to get involved with a food market in Washington, redevelopment of a warehouse in Philadelphia, affordable housing in Chicago's South Side, and a farm in the Hudson Valley in New York.

Very few developers—even those with a strong social mission—are aware of these opportunities to raise grassroots capital. You might encourage developers in your community to open up some of their projects to local investors. Point out that this gives them an entirely new source of capital for affordable multifamily housing, for land trusts, and for farm preservation. In small communities struggling to protect their downtowns, they might create one real estate vehicle for key parcels and get residents to buy pieces of the property.

My own fantasy is to create a neighborhood real estate investment trust that encourages neighbors to invest in one another's houses. This way, the superior performance of homeownership investments (outlined previously) can be shared with more people in the community. And with more homeownership, communities typically have less crime, better public health, and stronger schools. Why not start an entity like this in your own community?

Strategy 10: Invest in Local Government Projects

Interested in investing in local roads, bridges, ports, and convention centers? Or perhaps a new museum in town? Or your city's new high-speed Internet network? You might consider investing in municipal bonds. Local governments in the United States borrow money all the time, especially for expensive capital projects. Historically, municipal bonds have been attractive to investors because federal law makes the interest paid on many of them tax free.[28] When a local government puts all its assets on the line, these bonds are called "general obligation bonds." When it commits to paying bondholders only through project income—like tolls from a bridge—they are called "revenue bonds."

In 2015, a company called Neighborly introduced the concept of "civic microbonds" to lower the minimum denomination for investors. For the next four years it worked with cities, especially smaller ones, to help them issue bonds that could be marketed directly to residents. If your city wanted to upgrade the zoo, for example, it could issue zoo bonds for resident purchase. Neighborly recently shifted to focus on building municipal fiber-optic networks, but I suspect that other competitors will soon enter the microbond space.

Increasingly, cities are funding intriguing solar energy or stormwater management projects through grassroots investing. And for cities that have limited cash and have many residents who are reluctant to pay more taxes, this opens up a whole new potential revenue stream.

The key to bonds is that they require an offsetting stream of revenue in the future, either from the taxpayers or from project revenues. You cannot just issue bonds for teachers' salaries, unless the city is prepared to cover those costs in the future. But solar projects may mean the city does not have to build a new powerplant or grid connections to new neighborhoods. In Maryland, where the federal government is threatening to fine all counties that don't improve their stormwater management (because the current practices are poisoning the Chesapeake Bay), *avoiding* a multimillion-dollar fine could qualify as a revenue stream.

Another emerging type of local-government investment opportunity is called the social impact bond. This is a new idea, with only a couple of real-world examples. Suppose your local government wanted to invest in schools in a low-income neighborhood but didn't have the tax dollars to do this now. You also know that if you invest in kids early—through good education, school lunch programs, family support—there's a much lower chance of these kids going to prison. You might do a calculation that every dollar your community invests in these good things today prevents spending $20 to cover prison costs down the road. This logic convinced Goldman Sachs—yes, *that* Goldman Sachs—to issue social bonds. The bonds paid for education today, and they pay off if prison costs go down in the future.

For some critics, this is not very sound social policy. When you're betting on just one outcome with very little information about whether your bet will pay off, it really is little more than gambling. And while you could use your DIY Account to invest in things like this, the option may be too risky. But I suspect that more convincing social bonds will be developed by local governments loath to raise taxes.

Strategy 11: Invest in Local Investment Funds

Most of us do not have the time, expertise, or patience to find and evaluate one-off investments. That's why we typically rely on pools of capital, where someone else—a fund manager—is doing all the homework. A pool of investments also provides diversification, which lowers the risk of losing money. There are thousands of pools of capital in the United States looking for investors, and they go by the names of angel funds, venture capital funds, and hedge funds. Unfortunately, almost all of them are strictly for accredited investors and do not invest in local businesses or projects.

It's also worth pointing out that venture funds are particularly dangerous for local business and local well-being. These funds typically acquire 10–20 businesses, some of which start out as locally owned. But once the acquisition takes place, the venture fund assumes ownership and control. The few businesses that do exceptionally well—what they often hope is the next Microsoft—are "taken public" through an initial public offering (IPO), which destroys local ownership permanently. The rest, the failures, are quietly put to sleep. Either way, local businesses rarely survive the "help" given by venture capitalists.

For a grassroots investor, there *are* funds readily available for your money—mutual funds, insurance funds, pension funds—but almost all of them are 99.9 percent invested in global companies. True, some of the nearly 9,000 mutual funds enable you to invest in pools of municipal bonds, but good luck trying to find a pool of municipal bonds for a specific community, state, or region. Perhaps the best you can find are a handful of mutual funds that invest in notes from community development financial institutions (CDFIs) around the country. Praxis Mutual Funds, for example, commits about 1 percent of each of its funds to CDFIs, but to the disappointment of local investors, there's again no geographic targeting.

A word about CDFIs: In the 1990s, President Bill Clinton created a program to support federally licensed CDFIs with federal grants, loans, and loan guarantees. The idea was, and remains, that if a financial institution is focused on low-income neighborhoods or on businesses led by women or minorities, the government will help expand its capital. Among those institutions that qualify are community development corporations (CDCs), banks, credit unions, and loan funds. Unaccredited investors rarely invest in CDFIs. Generally, these institutions rely on funds from government agencies, foundations, and wealthy individuals.

The Calvert Foundation has made it possible for unaccredited investors to invest as little as $20 in CDFIs through its Community Investment Notes. To date, almost $450 million in notes have been issued, paying 1–4 percent, depending on how long the notes are held (fifteen-year purchases pay the best). But Calvert doesn't invest locally per se. Instead, it tries to focus its national pool of investment dollars on regional CDFIs more or less in proportion to where its investors live. Other funds open to unaccredited investors that support community-friendly enterprises across the country—but not in one place—are the Cooperative Fund of New England, RSF Social Finance, and the Shared Capital Cooperative.

What's most worth your attention is the expanding number of truly local investment funds. (See Chart 3.) These funds place money from local investors into a portfolio of local businesses or projects. For example, if you live in Western Massachusetts, you might think about investing in PVGrows Investment Fund (the PV stands for the Pioneer Valley). Since 2015, it has raised $2 million from investors and provided loans to thirty-five local food businesses. One beneficiary has been Mycoterra Farm, a producer of gourmet and medicinal specialty mushrooms, which was able to use its loan from the fund to convert an old horse stable into a new growing facility. "Community Investors" who put $1,000 to $10,000 into the fund for five years get a 2 percent rate of return. "Patient Capital Investors" who put in $10,000 to $250,000 for eight years get a 4 percent rate of return.

Because these funds are small and tend to focus on struggling businesses that require costly technical assistance, they pay relatively low returns—in the range of 2–4 percent per year. But as these funds expand and learn how to manage local portfolios better, I suspect their returns will creep closer and closer to the magical 5 percent target. If you want to start your own community investment fund, you can download a free handbook I just coauthored on the topic.[29]

Chart 3. Community Investment Funds Open to Unaccredited Investors

FUND NAME	LOCATION	FOCUS
Boston Impact Initiative Fund	Boston, MA	Businesses with an Economic-Justice Mission
Boston Ujima Fund	Boston, MA	Entrepreneurs of Color
Community Vision Lending	San Francisco, CA	Community Enterprises in California
East Bay Permanent Real Estate Cooperative	Oakland, CA	Affordable Housing
Economic Community Development Institute	Columbus, OH	Local Businesses
Iroquois Valley Farmland REIT	Evanston, IL	Organic Farms in 14 States
Mountain BizWorks	Asheville, NC	Local Businesses
New Hampshire Community Loan Fund	Concord, NH	Small Businesses in New Hampshire
New York City Real Estate Investment Cooperative	New York, NY	Affordable Housing
Northeast Kingdom Prosperity Fund	St. Johnsbury, VT	Small Businesses in NE Vermont
NorthEast Investment Cooperative	St. Paul, MN	Affordable Housing
PVGrows Investment Fund	North Deerfield, MA	Food Businesses in the Pioneer Valley
Runway Project	Oakland, CA	Local Entrepreneurs of Color
Vermont Community Loan Fund	Burlington, VT	Small Businesses in Vermont

Strategy 12: Invest in Your Local Bank or Credit Union

If you cannot find viable options among the strategies I've presented thus far, your last resort—almost always available—is not to put your money under a pillow. Instead, deposit it in a local bank or credit union. This is effectively a local investment, because we know that money deposited in one of these institutions is much more likely to be loaned to local business.

You might be interested in knowing that this is exactly what some foundations and cities have done. Confluence Philanthropy recommends its foundation members support local business, move their business into local banks, and until a better investment is found, put uncommitted funds on deposit in those banks.[30] Similarly, the cities of Phoenix and Tucson have begun moving their money into local banks, with explicit agreement that the money be used to support local businesses. Practically speaking, if you set up your DIY Account at a local bank or credit union—and there's no reason why you can't—you're doing this anyway.

The downside of doing this, of course, is that you will get very little return on your investment. This reflects the very low level of risk you are assuming. You get paid a guaranteed, but low, interest rate, and if the bank gets robbed or burns down, your account is fully insured by the federal government. Some believe that the era of super-low interest rates, however, may be ending, which would translate into higher interest payments by banks and credit unions. But as Mark Twain once said, "Prophecy is a good line of business, but it is full of risks."

A few banks and credit unions offer more interesting local investment opportunities, and many of these have actually been started because of initiatives led by depositors. Back in the 1980s, the E. F. Schumacher Society in Western Massachusetts convinced their local bank, then Great Barrington Savings (now Berkshire Bank), to set up a special account for supporting local businesses with small, $3,000–$5,000 loans. Depositors' money was at risk, but almost all the businesses paid back their loans.

Another example comes from Boston, where Equal Exchange, a fair-trade coffee company, convinced their local bank, then Wainwright Bank (now Eastern Bank), to set up a special certificate of deposit (CD) for fair-trade companies. The bank cleverly used this to recruit all kinds of new customers who wanted to do good things with their money. Their money is at risk, but thus far investors have gotten a steady stream of interest payments. And Equal Exchange wound up with a $1 million line of credit.

Again, none of these investments pay a Wall Street rate of return. But in principle, these bank instruments could ask for higher interest payments from the beneficiary businesses, which in turn would translate into a better rate of return to investors.

The Bottom Line

If the goal is to beat the 5 percent return that Wall Street stocks return, you have plenty of options. (See summary box.) Probably the best bets are those you control, such as investments in yourself, your kids, and your neighbors.

An Overview of Local Investment Options

Investing in Yourself, Friends, Family, or Neighbors

- Eliminate Credit Card Debt*
- Eliminate Student Debt*
- Become a Homeowner*
- Pay Off Your Mortgage*
- Reduce Energy and Other Household Bills*

Investing in Other Enterprises

- Cooperatives*
- Local For-Profits
- Local Non-Profits
- Local Real Estate*
- Municipal Bonds
- Community Investment Funds

Depositing Funds at a Local Bank, Thrift, or Credit Union

Other Options (sometimes local and sometimes open to unaccredited investors)

- Microcredit Funds
- Community Development Financial Institutions (CDFIs)
- Community Development Corporations (CDCs)
- Investment Clubs

(* = likely to generate a higher return than Wall Street)

But if you shop around, you should be able to find local co-ops, businesses, nonprofits, real estate projects, municipal bonds, and investment funds that can potentially deliver this level of return as well. Even if you can find only 3 percent or 4 percent deals, if you value your social rate of return at 1 percent or 2 percent, you will be beating Wall Street.

The only local investment option that will guarantee you a lower return is leaving your money in a local bank or credit union. If you are extremely averse to risk or cannot find other local investment opportunities, this is your default. The money then can sit, safe and insured, until you figure out a better use for it.

5

INTRODUCING DIY ACCOUNTS

To recap the previous chapters: Faced with two investment opportunities, one local and the other not, each expected to deliver the same return and carrying the same risk, you should always choose the local investment, because you will enjoy a social return on top of your private return. That said, there are many local investment options that will pay more than Wall Street and carry less risk, and these opportunities are likely to expand significantly in the years ahead. Given that, why are you not investing locally right now? The answer is probably that your life savings, if you have any, are locked up in your retirement accounts, in your workplace 401k, or in an IRA you set up years ago. How can you tap these funds to improve your life?

The DIY Accounts are your knights in shining armor. To use them for local investment, there are simple steps you must follow, each of which is covered in subsequent chapters. This chapter will give you the 30,000-foot view.

What Exactly Are DIY Accounts?

The term "DIY Accounts" has no legal significance. It's just my shorthand to lump together the two best tools you can use to invest tax-deferred dollars locally: the Self-Directed Individual Retirement Account and the Solo 401k. Even though these tools are different, they can be lumped together as DIY ("Do It Yourself") because they are used to accomplish the same purposes, and most of the rules governing them are the same. They also differ from other investment tools. Normally you must work through a conventional investment advisor or broker who will insist that you invest in Wall Street securities. With DIY Accounts, you make all the key decisions and can choose to invest locally.

Let's take a step back and review the universe of federally approved savings instruments you probably are already using. (See Chart 4.) One of their key characteristics is that they allow you to defer paying income taxes on your savings. They encourage you to save primarily for retirement but also for other emergencies that might come later in life. You can create your own Individual Retirement Account (IRA), or your employer can set up one for you—a 401k if you work for a for-profit company and a 403b for a non-profit. You are taxed only when you begin to withdraw the funds in retirement.

By deferring taxes, you can save substantial money over your lifetime. You can reinvest the money in your account again and again with no taxes due as your money grows exponentially. Another advantage is that typically when you retire, your income is lower than when you earned the money. Deferring taxes thus usually means paying taxes at a lower tax rate.

Chart 4. Commonly Used Tax-Deferred Savings Instruments

PLAN NAME	FOR WHOM	ROTH VERSION ALLOWED
Individual Retirement Account (IRA)	Anyone	Yes
401k	Employees with For-Profits	Yes
403b	Employees with Nonprofits	Yes
Thrift Savings Plan (TSP)	Federal Employees	Yes
Savings Incentive Match Plan for Employees (SIMPLE) IRA	Small Businesses	No
SIMPLE 401k	Small Businesses	Yes
Simplified Employee Pension (SEP) IRA	Small Businesses Self-Employees	No
529	College Savings	Operates like a Roth
Coverdell	Education Savings if Lower Income	Operates like a Roth
Health Savings Accounts (HSAs)	High-Deductible Health Insurance Plan Holders	No
Tax Deferred Savings Bonds	Interest-Free Series EE or Series I	No

Another type of retirement savings plan is called a "Roth," named for the sponsor of the 1997 legislation creating it, Senator William Roth of Delaware. With the Roth IRA, you pay taxes on the full amount now but then all the subsequent gains you access upon retirement are tax free. Private companies can set up a Roth 401k that operates by the same principle. The law has recently changed to allow savers to convert their regular IRAs and 401ks into Roth instruments by paying the taxes owed at the moment of conversion.

Breaking Up with Wells Fargo In Chicago

Camille Kerr, thirty-five, is a true believer in worker co-ops and now runs her own consulting business in Chicago to assist them. Earlier in her career, she worked at the National Center for Employee Ownership, which provided her with a retirement plan that generously matched her contributions. Oddly, even at a nonprofit committed to co-ops, all the investment choices were Fortune 500 companies. She was frustrated the plan did not give her the ability to invest in something she believed in. By the time she left the Center, she had accumulated $20,000.

"I knew that, eventually, I would need to figure out what to do with the funds," she recalls, "but did not want to deal with it immediately. After all, they were 'responsibly' invested in mutual funds, and I wasn't aware of anything I could do with the money except roll it into a traditional IRA. Since I did not have the interest or energy to go out of my way to support any particular publicly traded companies, I was likely going to put the money back into mutual funds anyway.

"When I switched jobs again in 2016, I thought about that retirement account again. By that point, I had heard about people investing in the Cooperative Fund of New England, the Local Enterprise Assistance Fund, or in the Shared Capital Cooperative, all funds that lent to worker cooperatives. I started the process of setting up a Self-Directed IRA, but when I realized I would have to get paperwork from my former employer, my motivation fizzled. My new work was demanding, I was juggling a lot of personal changes, and I didn't feel like I had the capacity to deal with it.

"When I left that job to start my own consulting firm . . . I finally felt ready to commit to the process. I had recently broken up with Wells Fargo as part of the move to live in line with my values. I had also witnessed example after example where capital access played a critical role in whether a worker cooperative initiative ultimately succeeded or failed. It felt like an imperative to move my money."

She decided to set up a Self-Directed IRA. She reached out to Christina Jennings, the executive director of the Shared Capital Cooperative, to ask for advice on how to invest in their fund. Christina quickly sent back some investment options and recommended Union Bank & Trust in Minneapolis as Camille's Self-Directed IRA provider.

"The process involved a lot of paperwork," Camille says, "but didn't take more than a few hours of my time total. The forms included a distribution form from the retirement plan administrator of my former employer, a custodial agreement, a money market election for any funds that aren't actively invested, an account application, a tax withholding form, and a couple other odds and ends. Altogether, it took approximately two months to set up—and most of that time was the custodian processing the paperwork I submitted."

Camille put most of her savings into the Shared Capital Cooperative, in a long-term equity investment with a target annual dividend of 5 percent. She just received her first 5 percent payout. She also made a few smaller, riskier investments in an entrepreneurship hub in Englewood, a distressed neighborhood in Chicago.

Camille's only regret is that The Next Egg was not around when she was choosing her provider. Had she had the full list of providers and their prices, she could have shrunk her annual fees from $600 to perhaps half that amount. Now that she has her own business, she's thinking about setting up her own Solo 401k, perhaps jointly owned by her partner. "That said, I encourage people to be bold with their investments. Don't be foolish, but if we want a New Economy, patient capital from us will be critical."

There are other kinds of instruments out there as well, but for simplicity, I will not be focusing on them in the rest of the book. For example, small businesses can set up a Simplified Employee Pension (SEP) IRA or a Savings Incentive Match Plan for Employees (SIMPLE) IRA, both of which allow much higher annual contributions. These instruments have special sets of rules concerning who can set up the accounts, how much you can save each year, and when you can access the funds. Like IRAs, most outside firms that offer these tools do not give you any local investment options.

The IRS also lets you set up special savings accounts for education and health care. Coverdell Education Savings Accounts (CESAs), which are structured like Roth IRAs, allow you to squirrel away funds for your kids' college education. Health Savings Accounts (HSAs) allow those of us opting for health plans with very high deductibles to apply tax-deferred savings to future medical expenses. Both these tools, by the way, can be invested locally like the other DIY Accounts.

The most important characteristic of all the DIY Accounts is that you get to choose where you put your money. By expanding your investment options, you can increase your returns, lower your risks, and benefit your community.

What Are the Features of Regular IRAs and 401ks?

To understand the DIY Accounts, let's begin with the basics of vanilla-flavored IRAs and 401ks. A typical IRA, provided by thousands of institutions, allows you to set up an account, put away money tax deferred every year, and withdraw funds when you retire. Here are some of the key rules:

- *Contribution*—Practically speaking, you can contribute $6,000 per year. If you are earning less than $6,000 in a year, you can contribute as much of your earnings as you like. If you are over fifty, you can contribute another $1,000 per year.

- *Withdrawal*—Since the whole purpose of the IRA is to encourage savings for retirement, you should not touch the money until you turn at least fifty-nine-and-a-half years old. At that point, you can start making withdrawals, and the gains are taxed as ordinary income.

- *Early Withdrawals*—The way the IRS discourages savers from raiding their funds early is to penalize early withdrawals. Take out money early and you must pay a penalty of 10 percent to the IRS (in addition to ordinary income taxes).

- *Later Retirement*—The IRS allows you to continue saving until age seventy and a half. Beyond that point, the IRS has required minimum distributions (RMDs) that must be withdrawn from your accounts each year.[1]

- *Rollover*—You are allowed to roll over an IRA into most other kinds of tax-deferred retirement vehicles, including a Self-Directed IRA and a Solo 401k. As long as these transfers are executed properly within sixty days, your savings remain untaxed.

- *Personal Control*—Throughout this process, you control how the funds are invested—kind of. The financial institution holding your IRA will present you with a bunch of investment options, usually mutual funds with stocks and bonds linked with Wall Street firms. *None of these investment opportunities will be local.*

A 401k is a retirement account set up by your employer. Instead of you entering a relationship with another financial institution, your employer does. One advantage of a 401k over an IRA is that your annual contributions can be significantly greater—up to $19,000 per year, plus another $6,000 if you are above the age of fifty. Many employers sweeten this deal by matching—dollar for dollar, sometimes even two for one or more—your contributions up to a certain ceiling.

The downside of the 401k is that it stays with your employer throughout your work tenure. Your employer usually will not let you touch it until you resign, are fired, or retire. Moreover, your employer will restrict your ability to roll over your 401k into another tax-deferred instrument. But according to the IRS, nearly two in three 401k plans allow for what is called an "in-service withdrawal."[2] In additional to withdrawals for disability and financial hardship, these plans may allow in-service rollovers to employees who reach the age of fifty-nine and a half. If you have a 401k plan, check with your employer to see what your rights are.

The DIY Accounts are really just slightly altered versions of the IRA and the 401k. The main difference is that you have a much broader range of investment opportunities. In fact, it's easier to list what you cannot invest in than what you can. We will take a deep dive into the no-go list later in Chapter 9, but for now, let's just say you can't invest in highly speculative things (like coins) or in your own business or home (or your kids' businesses or homes). But other than that, your options are wide open.

To open a Self-Directed IRA, you need to find a special institution that offers the service. These are primarily licensed trust companies, along with a few banks and credit unions. They will assign you a custodian who handles all the practical and legal requirements for running your account. You make all the investment decisions yourself and let your custodian know about them through a bunch of forms, and provided they are legally kosher, the custodian, as your trustee, must carry them out.

Since the custodian performs a lot more work than occurs in a typical IRA, you will have to pay for this service. My colleagues at The Next Egg have reviewed the cost packages from dozens of companies, some as low as several hundred dollars per year and others as high as several thousand dollars per year.[3] Some IRA custodians charge low annual fees but lard on additional fees for certain kinds of transactions—say, complex real estate deals. *You therefore must shop around to find a custodian who is right for you.*

A Solo 401k is designed exclusively for self-employed individuals. The whole purpose of establishing the Solo 401k was to give millions of self-employed Americans the ability to save for their retirement as easily as an employee of a company could. But if you have a day job and run another business on the side, you also can set up a Solo 401k. A list of some of the best providers of Solo 401ks is provided in Chart 5.

There are several advantages a Solo 401k has over a Self-Directed IRA:

- *Checkbook Control*—Unlike your Self-Directed IRA, where your custodian controls the checkbook, you control it instead. You open your own account at your favorite bank, duly registering it in the name of your trust (not you), and then you are in the driver's seat. That also means, of course, that you must know how to obey the rules.

- *Lower Expense*—Since you are running the show, you don't need to pay a Self-Directed IRA custodian any annual expenses. There are small expenses you may need to pay each year to purchase an IRS-approved plan, but these are typically just a few hundred dollars.

Chart 5. A Partial List of Community-Friendly Solo 401k Providers[4]

PROVIDER	FIRST YEAR FEE	SUBSEQUENT YEAR FEES	WEBSITE	PHONE
AccuPlan	$995	$275	www.accuplan.net	602-312-5790
American IRA	$50	$450	www.americanira.com	828-257-4949
Broad Financial	$995	$149	www.broadfinancial.com	800-395-5200
Discount Solo 401k	$575	$100	www.discountsolo401k.com	303-427-4519
Entrust Group	$50	$399	www.theentrustgroup.com	800-392-9653
Equity Trust	$600	0.15% Assets	www.trustetc.com	888-382-4727
IRA Financial Group	$899	$199	www.irafinancialgroup.com	888-472-0649
My Solo 401k Financial	$550	$125	www.mysolo401k.net	800-489-7571
Navigator Business & Retirement Services	$495	$300	www.sdirahandbook.com	602-761-9798
QPS	$500	$350	www.qpscentral.com	303-952-5066
Revzon	$350	$250	www.revzonconsulting.com	877-254-7085
Rocket Dollar	$360	$180	www.rocketdollars.com	502-439-3233
Sense Financial	$1,000	$200	www.sensefinancial.com	949-228-9394
Solo 401k by Nabers Group	$399	$99	www.nabers.com	877-903-2220
Solo 401k Services	$595	$99	www.solo401kservices.com	800-614-1652

- *Lending*—If you prepare your plan properly, you can make a low-interest loan to yourself of up to $50,000 or 50 percent of your account, whichever is less. And there are no limits on how you can use that loan! You could use it for a down payment on a house or to pay off high-interest credit cards—the invest-in-yourself options discussed in the previous chapter. You just need to pay yourself back within five years in at least quarterly installments with an interest rate of prime plus 1 percent (as of today, that's just over 5 percent). To be clear, the interest payment effectively enlarges your retirement account. *Please note that this kind of loan to yourself would be illegal in a Self-Directed IRA.*

- *Large Annual Contributions*—The Solo 401k effectively allows you to make not one but two annual contributions: one as an employee and one as an employer. Just like a regular 401k, you can contribute up to $19,000 per year as an employee of yourself ($25,000 if you are fifty or older). But as your own employer, you also can contribute up to $37,000. That means that your annual contribution can be $56,000—or $62,000 if you are fifty or older. That's almost ten times greater than the annual limit for your Self-Directed IRA!

You also can have both a Self-Directed IRA and a Solo 401k. For most people, however, $56,000 is the cap on your total contribution to all your retirement accounts in a tax year ($62,000 if you are fifty or older). Given that, you might as well use just one instrument instead of two or more to keep down your annual costs and administrative work.

But if you have an exceptionally good year and you want to put away more money, another loophole is available. Remember, your spouse can do the same thing as you do. You and your spouse can be co-owners of a limited liability company (LLC) that serves as your shared self-employment business, and each of you can claim the maximum contribution. That means your family can tuck away a maximum of $112,000 per year (or $124,000 if you are both over age fifty). And there are some circumstances in which you can contribute even more.[5] Again, all of this is possible only with a Solo 401k.

What Are the Key Steps for DIY Investing?

The chapters ahead will show you, step by step, how to fully deploy your DIY Accounts for local investing.

- How to set up an account with either of the DIY Accounts (Chapter 6).

- How to find local investment opportunities (Chapter 7).

- How to select the opportunities most appropriate for you, weighing the likely risks and returns (Chapter 8).

- How to make sure your investment choices are allowable under the law and stay far away from the danger zone (Chapter 9).

- How to administer your DIY Accounts with the right forms and a smart withdrawal strategy (Chapter 10).

- Finally, we'll talk about the future. The local investment revolution is changing things pretty fast, and you need to be ready for it (Chapter 11).

The Bottom Line

All things being equal, a Solo 401k will give you many more options than a Self-Directed IRA. You can save significantly more money each year. You can make loans to yourself. You can control your own checkbook. And the fees are much lower. But you do have to do more work and be more mindful of the rules. (See summary in Chart 6.)

Chart 6. Self-Directed IRA vs. Solo 401k: An Overview

	SELF-DIRECTED IRA	SOLO 401K
Who Can Set Up?	Any Adult	Any Self-Employed Adult (even if employed elsewhere)
Maximum Annual Contribution?	$6,000 $7,000 (if over 50)	$56,000 $62,000 (if over 50)
Do You Need to Hire a Custodian?	Yes, Unless You Set Up a Checkbook LLC	No
Can You Loan Yourself Money?	No	Yes (the lesser of 50% of your account or $50,000)
Can You Decide Where to Invest?	Yes (provided your custodian agrees it's legal)	Yes
Lowest Annual Cost?	$350	$300
Can You Make This a Roth Account?	Yes	Yes
Can You Roll Over Other Pension Savings Accounts into This Account?	Yes for IRAs Yes for 401ks after You Retire, Resign, or Are Fired	Yes for IRA (no for Roth IRAs) Yes for 401ks after You Retire, Resign, or Are Fired

6

SETTING UP YOUR
ACCOUNT

Your first decision is this: Which DIY option do you want? All things being equal, you will want a Solo 401k. Why? Because you can truly do it all yourself, at a lower expense. You create a special checking account for your Solo 401k, add funds each year, and write checks to make your own investments. If you don't qualify for a Solo 401k, then you must turn to the Self-Directed IRA. For that option, you must hire a custodian, which requires time and money—though if you're smart about it, not a lot of either.

How Can You Qualify for a Solo 401k?

There are two very simple requirements for a Solo 401k: You must have at least one dollar of reported self-employment income, and you must not have any full-time employees.[1] That's it!

For the income requirement, you don't need a dollar of net income to adopt a Solo 401k plan—just a dollar of gross income. (Of course, if you don't have net income, you won't be able to make a contribution that year.) If you are self-employed, your income includes wages, salaries, tips, and all kinds of earnings from your self-employment activities. Your net income is what you have left after deducting proper business expenses and self-employment taxes for Social Security and Medicare.

Even if you hold a full-time job and have a consulting business on the side, you can set up a Solo 401k for the consultancy. You just need to report self-employment income properly on your taxes. Most self-employed individuals report income and expenses on Schedule C of their 1040 tax form. That's the default. It's where you report the business activity of your own LLC. You are also considered self-employed as a partner in a partnership or as a member in an LLC owned by multiple members.

You need to generate income through work. For example, if you rent property, your status will depend on whether you get income passively or generate it actively. If you just receive a check from a tenant every month, whether the tenant lives in your own house or in another property you own, that's probably passive income—and you would report that on Schedule E. If you also provide regular services to your property or run your own property management company, that would fit more squarely into Schedule C. If you report your income on Schedule C, remember again that you will have to pay self-employment tax on it—and what's left over will dictate what you can invest in your Solo 401k.

If your business has part-time employees, you still may be able to set up a Solo 401k plan. The tricky issue here, however, is how the IRS defines "full-time." According to the IRS, a full-time employee must work at least one thousand hours per year. To put this in perspective, a person who works forty hours per week for fifty-two weeks logs 2,080 hours. That means that even someone on payroll twenty hours per week will be deemed "full time." But less than that and you're good!

If you and your spouse jointly own a business and both work for it, your spouse will not be considered an employee. Couples do this all the time.

If you run a company with a bunch of employees and also have a side consulting business, you still can set up a Solo 401k for the side business—with one proviso: You can't set up a side business just to avoid setting up a pension plan for your employees in your main company. Whenever you have employees, you must observe the Employment Retirement Income Security Act of 1974, also known as ERISA. Under this federal law, you don't have to provide pension benefits to your employees, but if you do, there are many complicated and expensive rules to follow. One of them is that similar benefits must be offered to similar classes of employees. If you give yourself a pension plan, you will have to make it available to all other managers.

You can't circumvent the rules by setting up a company on the side and making yourself the sole employee. Nor can you set up a group of companies to sneak around the rules because of what the IRS calls "controlled group" rules. If you own 80 percent or more of a company, you cannot set up another company with different pension rules. "You," in this case, means not just you but all your lineal descendants, your parents, and your spouse. It doesn't matter how the companies are structured—for example, whether Company A is a parent to Company B, or Company A and B are equals. If 80 percent of the companies are owned by five or fewer shareholders, they are considered one big company for pension purposes, and each class of employees must be given identical pension plans.

The Test Pilot in California

Before The Next Egg was launched, one of the founding organizations, the Sustainable Economies Law Center (SELC) in Oakland, was looking for someone to take a Solo 401k on a test flight. Sue Bennett, fifty-seven, happily volunteered. Unlike most of her younger colleagues, she actually had accumulated some significant retirement savings with previous employers, such as the East Bay Community Foundation. SELC agreed to cover her costs for two years and make its attorneys available to answer all her questions.

Sue obtained a Solo 401k plan from Sense Financial for $1,000 (subsequent years are $200). Even though she had accumulated $95,000 in two 401ks, she decided to put only $4,000 into the plan. She is still looking for good places to park her money. For starters, she put $1,000 into the East Bay Permanent Real Estate Cooperative, which is a community investment fund created by SELC to promote affordable housing. She will be paid a fixed interest rate over ten years. She also put $500 into Kiva loans to support a local catering microentrepreneur. She struggled over whether the loan met the legal standard of prudence, because Kiva pays back only principal, not interest. She decided that it was a reasonable investment, because she planned to hire the caterer from time to time. She has placed the rest of her funds in a money market account while she considers other options. Top of her list is California FarmLink, which is helping farmers acquire land and equipment.

Besides finding good investments, Sue's biggest challenge was finding a bank to set up her trust account. Fortunately, the Self-Help Federal Credit Union, which is all about local investment and innovation, has an office in Oakland and was happy to figure out a solution.

"I'm definitely feeling better about my investments now," Sue reports, "but I will need a lot more experience. I've invested only a small fraction of my savings thus far but am excited about the long term. I plan to move all my money into the Solo 401k, and to invest those funds in more ways that are of MY choosing."

How Can You Set Up a Solo 401k?

Keep in mind is that you, the boss, are basically setting up a pension plan for your business, even though it's just for the benefit of you. You need to follow these steps:

- *Plan*—You should design a plan that fits your needs. Most Solo 401k holders want to serve as their own trustee, to maintain checkbook control, and to be able to invest in a wide range of options.

- *Trust Agreement*—A 401k is a "trust," where a trustee temporarily holds the title of the property for another beneficiary. In the case of a Solo 401k, most people opt to serve as their own trustee. This requires a trustee agreement, which also can be incorporated into the written plan.

- *Summary*—You need a summary plan description (SPD) of its key features, written in plain English.

- *Resolution*—Your firm must craft and pass a resolution to adopt the plan. Those approving the plan will be just yourself if you are self-employed, all the members of your LLC, or all the partners in your partnership.

- *IRS Approval*—Every plan needs to be reviewed and approved by the IRS, which is communicated through an official acceptance letter.

You can write your own plan and submit it to the IRS for approval, but that's cumbersome and time consuming. You can get an accountant or law firm to write your plan from scratch, but that is expensive. That's why most people purchase pre-prepared, IRS-approved templates, or "prototypes" as they are called in the industry. Some prototypes are boilerplate documents that you must take as is, but others allow certain options to be added or subtracted. Prototype plans are usually provided with legally compliant summaries, adoption forms, and IRS approval letters.

See the adjacent box for a checklist of the features you will want to have in your Solo 401k prototype.

Some mainstream investment firms, like Schwab, allow you to set up a Solo 401k, but you need to be careful here. Many of these plans contain the same restrictions as regular

IRAs and 401ks and largely steer you toward Wall Street investments. It's better to start with the companies listed in Chart 5.

A Checklist for a Solo 401k Prototype

When you appoint yourself as trustee, you give yourself all the powers needed to run the Solo 401k. This usually includes the powers to

- Open a bank account.
- Receive funds.
- Invest funds per the beneficiary's instructions.
- Disburse funds as the beneficiary wishes.
- Consent, oppose, or participate in any contracts, leases, or service agreements.
- Settle or manage any lawsuits.
- Pay or renegotiate any debt.

For local investing, make sure you have the power to

- Appoint yourself as the trustee.
- Maintain control over the investment checkbook.
- Invest in a wide range of permissible local investment opportunities.
- Create a separate Roth account.
- Take a loan from the account.

A plan can have more than one trustee, if you want. This might make sense if spouses are both beneficiaries. If one dies before the other, the living spouse can then easily transfer the remaining assets. For example, suppose both spouses jointly owned a single LLC. When one spouse dies, the other can then easily transfer the assets. Having more than one trustee means that all the legal documents must be approved and signed by all the trustees.

How Can You Set Up a Self-Directed IRA?

If you cannot qualify for a Solo 401k or if you don't want to worry about getting the details right on your own, you should create a Self-Directed IRA. The main difference is that you are hiring someone else, a "custodian," to serve as the trustee instead of yourself.

The primary benefits are that some of the paperwork is lifted from you and there are fewer chances of making costly mistakes. A Solo 401k takes more work, though the whole purpose of this book is to help you keep this work to a minimum.

But there are disadvantages to opting for a Self-Directed IRA. For one, the annual cost may be higher. Moreover, not all custodians are alike. Some are more accessible than others. Some are pricier. Some will discourage or refuse to approve certain transactions you want. On top of an annual fee, some charge for every investment transaction, with surcharges for complicated transactions like property purchases.

The Bottom Line

To take advantage of a Solo 401k, you need to be self-employed, derive income from that enterprise, and have no employees. Your spouse can co-own this business and take advantage of this as well. The easiest way to set one up is to purchase an IRS-approved prototype plan that has all the features you want.

If you are not self-employed, then you should set up a Self-Directed IRA. Find a company that provides the service and hire a custodian you like who will do most of the work for you.

Under either option, you remain in the driver's seat when it comes to choosing the investments you want—including the option to invest locally.

7

IDENTIFYING
LOCAL INVESTMENT
OPPORTUNITIES

O nce you have a DIY Account, how will you use it? What local investment opportunities can you find, and how exactly will you find them? The question is not unlike the one Alice in Wonderland put to the Cheshire Cat:

> "Would you tell me, please, which way I ought to go from here?"
>
> "That depends a good deal on where you want to get to," said the Cat.
>
> "I don't much care where—" said Alice.
>
> "Then it doesn't matter which way you go," said the Cat.
>
> "—so long as I get *somewhere*," Alice added as an explanation.
>
> "Oh, you're sure to do that," said the Cat, "if you only walk long enough."

This chapter lays out eight steps for your long walk and concludes with a radical solution if you're still stumped: Use your DIY Account to start your own business.

Eight Steps to Finding Promising Local Investments

Believe it or not, local investment opportunities are all around you, even if you can't see them yet. We're a bit like a fish that never knows it's swimming in water. You must train your senses to notice the myriad possibilities in your community. Here are eight sure-fire steps to find what you're looking for.

Step 1: Start with Yourself

One reason I dwelled on opportunities to invest in yourself in Chapter 4 is because this is where most Americans are seriously underinvested. It's where smart local investments—in reducing credit card balances, eliminating student debt, becoming a homeowner, paying off the mortgage faster, and tightening your energy efficiency—will have the greatest returns with the lowest risks. I doubt you have exhausted all these opportunities. Which ones make the most sense for you?

Remember, however, that the only legal way you can use your DIY Accounts to invest in yourself is by making yourself a loan through your Solo 401k. You cannot use a Self-Directed IRA for this. And with the Solo 401k, you're also limited to loaning yourself the lesser of $50,000 or half your savings. That said, I suspect there's a lot of productive investment you could do in your life for $50,000.

If you don't have a Solo 401k but have other retirement savings, here's a simple suggestion. Set up an account on eBay to resell junk in your closet. You don't need a business license or a business name. You don't need an expensive infrastructure. Just be sure you have a few dollars of gross income to report on Schedule C, and then you have the legal right to open a Solo 401k. Once that's available, roll your other retirement accounts into the Solo 401k as soon as you can and *then* proceed to make a loan to yourself.

Step 2: Investigate Your Family's Needs

Next, ask the same questions you just asked yourself about other members of your family. Do your kids have credit card or student debt? Do they need a house? Could they use a solar-electric system to reduce their heating bills? Again, your kids are disqualified recipients of DIY Account funds, *except* if you do this through a loan to yourself.

That said, as I detail in Chapter 9, lots of people in your life are not disqualified. Your brother and sister, your nieces and nephews, your friends, your neighbors—as far as the IRS is concerned, you can put 100 percent of your DIY Accounts into them. Next Thanksgiving, why not have a serious financial conversation with these folks?

Suppose you have a friend, Ed, who is buying a home and needs $10,000 for a down payment. You could use your DIY Account to lend Ed the money. If Ed wants to replace high-interest credit cards with a lower-interest loan from your DIY Account, you could also do that—and this could generate huge benefits for both you and Ed. Maybe the best rate of return you could find on other local investments is 6 percent per year from your co-op's capital project. Ed is now paying 25 percent per year in interest on his credit cards. You two could strike a deal for 15 percent, and both of you would be huge winners.

It's worth adding that you need to be careful with people you don't know very well (and sometimes with people you know all too well!): Ed can default, and your legal recourse will depend on your agreement. If Ed has high credit-card debt, that may be a sign he's already in financial trouble— so you'll want to learn more about why he thinks he will have the funds in the near future to pay off the loan before you engage in a transaction like this. Creative local investment choices invite family members, friends, and neighbors to have more honest (if difficult) conversations with one another about their financial needs. You may be surprised by how many people who you assumed were in great financial shape would welcome your help.

Step 3: Evangelize for Local Investment

Don't just wait for local investments to come your way— invite them! Talk with the managers of your co-op, your local bookstore owners, your church board, your favorite non-profit director, and see what their expansion plans are. Would it make sense for your business to have your own building instead of paying rent to a mercurial landlord? How about a second store? Let them know everything you've learned about local investment. If you convince them to make a securities offering, you'll be the first in line to take advantage of it.

Step 4: Find Fellow Travelers

You are probably not the first person in your community to get bitten by the local investment bug. You might ascertain whether any Slow Money members are in your area. Slow Money is one of the few national organizations in the United States promoting local investing, though principally in farms and local food businesses. It was started by an investor named Woody Tasch, who in 2008 wrote an influential book commonly referred to as *Slow Money*. Tasch was inspired by the Slow Food movement, which promotes a style of eating that is the opposite of fast food, emphasizing the quality of food rather than the quantity, the relationships around the table that develop through a leisurely pace, and the rewards that can come from close relationships with local farmers. There are now thousands of members and dozens of Slow Money chapters spread around the country. These people and chapters can share with you what they have learned about local investment.

In Ypsilanti, Michigan, a registered investment advisor named Angela Barbash, who runs a company called Revalue that we will learn more about in Chapter 8, has organized a regular call involving representatives from local banks, federally designated community development financial institutions (CDFIs), and community investment funds, as well as impact investors, to identify promising local businesses for their collective investment. They also share some of the due diligence and strategize about how to split opportunities among their clients. (Interestingly, local angel and venture capital investors were on the early calls and then dropped off, complaining that local businesses were of no interest!)

Check out the list in the adjacent box to see other people in your community who are likely to have information about companies, projects, or people seeking money.

People in Your Community Likely to Know Local Investment Opportunities

Local Government

- City Council Members Interested in Business Promotion
- Economic Developers
- Planners

Private Sector

- Angel Investors
- Bankers
- Broker-Dealers
- Community Development Corporations (CDCs)
- Community Development Financial Institutions (CDFIs)
- Community Foundations
- Registered Investment Advisors
- Venture Capitalists

Business Support Sector

- Business Schools
- Community College Entrepreneurship Programs
- Incubators and Accelerators
- Maker Spaces
- Shared Work Spaces

Step 5: Check the Crowdfunding Sites

There are now about three dozen federally licensed crowd-funding portals.[1] The largest among them are Republic, SeedInvest, StartEngine, and Wefunder. While you could go through these sites, one by one, and identify companies from your community, another terrific site called Investibule has already done this for you.

Investibule (*www.investibule.co*) is an online repository of listings on various crowdfunding sites started by Arno Hesse, a Slow Money organizer in California, and Amy Cortese, author of a pioneering book called *Locavesting*. They also include intrastate offerings and direct public offerings (DPOs). You can search by city or state (and soon by zip code), and you will instantly see what companies and projects in your region have gotten legal permission to raise money from grassroots investors.

Step 6: Unleash a LION

Ultimately, local investment is a relationship between an investor and an investee. So building a local ecosystem to facilitate local investing is about weaving these relationships. Remember, private offerings—that is, those that cannot be advertised generally—usually require a "preexisting relation-ship" between the offeror business and the offeree investor.

The Local Investing Opportunities Network (LION) was started by a group of eight citizens in Port Townsend, Washington, as a way to introduce local investors and busi-nesses to one another. Through periodic gatherings open to any interested investors or businesses, the group helps establish the "preexisting relationships" to facilitate local investment. As a result, more than seven million dollars of new local investment has been facilitated in the 10,000-person town from 2006 to 2016. Other chapters of LION have popped up around the country. If one doesn't exist in your town, you might consider starting one. Full details and best practices about how to do that are available at *www.local-investing.com.*

Step 7: Make A Public List

If you have any web ability at all, you might do your community a favor and put up a list of every local investment offering available. This is what I'm planning to do now with my colleague Stephanie Geller through what we call the Maryland Neighborhood Exchange. It's a website where we envision onboarding promising local businesses and encourage potential investors to become fans. Relationships ensue. Fans would help the businesses become stronger, and businesses accumulate names for future crowdfunding offers. We would not do any investment transactions ourselves but rather send businesses and investors to national crowdfunding sites like Wefunder and Honeycomb Credit. We would pay our bills through finders' fees and listing fees.

If it's too big a stretch to start your own web listing, you might encourage your city, your credit union, or a friendly registered investment advisor or broker-dealer to do so. (Note to finance professionals—this is a great new business opportunity!) One way of lightening the load is to team up with other interested people in your community to prepare such as list. You need to be mindful, as we are in the Maryland Neighborhood Exchange, that under current securities, you can only list "offers" that have either duly registered with federal and state securities departments or fit within a specific exemption from registration. But there's nothing illegal about creating a watch list of "great businesses seeking to expand."

Another form of a public list is a handbook of local investment options by type. I've prepared handbooks covering about two dozen options for the states of Vermont and Washington.[2] If you're interested in working together to produce handbooks for your own state, please let me know.

Once a web listing like this appears in your community, guess what happens next: Every person, project, or business looking for money will want to be listed!

Step 8: Form an Investment Club

Finally, you should think about joining a local investment club or creating one if nothing exists already. A small group of investors is allowed to come together, form their own LLC, pool their money, and then invest together. Everyone can direct their DIY Accounts to put money into the LLC. The key requirement is that every member has to be involved in every decision. You don't need consensus on every issue, just complete participation. That means you can't designate a leader to do all the work on everyone's behalf. Everyone must be active.

The virtue of being in a local investment club is that instead of your doing all the work to identify promising local investments, you can split the work among a dozen people. Plus you can split the challenging process of evaluating each opportunity, and you can work through difficult questions that come up about the DIY rules.

On the Learning Curve in Florida

Laura Oldanie, forty-nine, is a self-employed blogger based in St. Petersburg, Florida, who is trying to live a low-impact life in every respect, including her finances. After attending a Slow Money meeting in Northern California two years ago, she decided to set up a Self-Directed IRA and put three-quarters of her retirement savings in the account. By setting up a checkbook LLC, she effectively created her own local investment company, though she is still figuring out how to invest her funds.

For $50, she opened a Self-Directed IRA with Advanta, a company based near her, to support a local business with a solid reputation. She then hired a local attorney recommended by Advanta to set up the self-directed LLC for about $700, which covered attorney fees and the company's registration. Her annual fees are $295 per year for the Self-Directed IRA, and $140 for maintaining the LLC.

Thus far, she has made two local investments. One is a share of a permaculture farm not far from where she lives. The other local investment is in a friend who took over the management of a large organic farm in Tampa Bay. Laura made him a personal loan to help save the farm and expects to be paid back within a year. As far as she is concerned, "I'm putting my money in the world I'd like to live in."

Laura also has invested her money, though not locally, in StreetShares, based in Richmond, Virginia. StreetShares makes loans to veterans and their families to help them start and expand their own small businesses. Laura bought a bond that pays her a flat 5 percent per year.

She found other interesting nonlocal investments on the web. She bought stock in TerraCycle, which is helping to make containers reusable, directly through the company's website. And she spotted several other interesting companies on the crowdfunding platform Wefunder. Among them were Scrap Connection, which helps businesses buy and sell scrap materials; Urban Juncture, a food business in a distressed neighborhood in Chicago; and Ganaz, an app that improves farmers' management of and relationship with temporary workers.

Her advice to others? "Investing through self-directed retirement accounts is completely doable! But it is important to educate yourself thoroughly before getting started. Read as many books as possible and ask lots of questions of custodian companies as well as account holders."

Is the Investment Opportunity Available to Only Accredited Investors?

As you collect information about potential local investments, one critical question you need to ask is this: Will it accept investment from grassroots investors?

Let's review our earlier discussion of this basic securities law concept: If you are wealthy, in the top 5 percent or so of the population as measured by your income or wealth, you are considered "accredited" and allowed to invest in almost anything, any time, no questions asked. The rest of us, what I have called "grassroots investors" and others call "retail investors," are, under the law, "unaccredited investors." That means that we can invest only in entities that have done the legal paperwork that allows us to invest.

We unaccredited investors must make sure the local business, nonprofit, municipal bond, real estate project, or investment fund we're interested in permits our participation. These entities will happily tell you, but it's additional homework for you. By law, they are not permitted to sell you securities unless they have gotten permission to do so through their legal filings or they are exempt from making such filings.

Some exemptions are crystal clear. There's no legal impediment against unaccredited investors investing in themselves or their families (though there are significant limits on how you can use Solo 401ks or Self-Directed IRAs for these purposes).

Investing in your neighbors is trickier. There's the "friends and family" exemption in securities law. As long as you have a strong "preexisting relationship" with someone, you can proceed with the deal. You need to be careful, however, because the contours of this exception vary from state to state. A Facebook buddy probably does not qualify as an exempt friend. Nor would someone who just moved in next door. But if you have known someone for some time and you have a friendship, why not?

Many people assume that even if they are unaccredited, they can team up with accredited investors and then access investment opportunities available only to accredited investors. Nope. Say you have an investment club. If your club has even one unaccredited investor, it can invest only in businesses that have done all the legal paperwork to accept money from unaccredited investors.

How Can You Finance Your Own Business?

If the eight steps I've covered do not generate enough opportunities, here's one last resort: Use your DIY Account to finance your own company. Surely you have had a dream business you always wanted to run. Maybe a café, bookstore, or theater? Mine is to create a moose petting zoo. My partner, now retired, dreams of training cheetahs. Whatever your passion, you must follow a bunch of rules to prevent your DIY Account from getting into hot water. *This option is probably not something to attempt unless you have reviewed the relevant documents with your attorney.*

The typical way to do this is to have your DIY Account set up a new limited liability company (LLC) with 100 percent of the membership held by your Account. All the founding and operational documents and the bank account must be in the name of the Account (for example, John Smith's Solo 401k), not your name (John Smith).

There are several reasons you might choose this kind of structure.

- First, you don't have to file any tax forms for the company.

- Second, by forming an LLC, you protect from liability yourself, your Account, and your custodian (if you have a Self-Directed IRA). This could be especially valuable if you are purchasing real estate to receive rental income. You put money into your DIY Account, your Account purchases the property, and the rental income flows into your Account, all duly insulated. Be mindful, however, that liability limits are imperfect shields. If there's a major liability and your Account cannot cover it, courts tend to treat your Account as a revocable trust—and may still hold you personally liable.[3]

- Third, if you have a Self-Directed IRA, the creation of an LLC gives you greater checkbook control over how your investments flow. (If you have a Solo 401k, you already have that control.) You don't have to rely just on your custodian. Through the LLC, you can make day-to-day decisions about the company. You can enter into contracts, sign checks, pay expenses, and so forth. When quick business decisions are required, it's smarter to have this kind of structure than to go through the time-consuming process of having the custodian handle all your administrative transactions.

If your Account has an LLC, there are important rules you need to follow. In Chapter 9, we're going to talk about "prohibited transactions," but the following pages offer some coming attractions. You cannot use your DIY Account to benefit yourself—as opposed to benefiting your Account. Even an incidental benefit to you is regarded as "self-dealing." Given this, the IRS once argued that creating an LLC was doing business with yourself and therefore prohibited. But a string of court cases has established that when the company has no shareholders, the act of your Account buying the entity outright is not doing business with yourself.[4]

You do not have to hire someone else to manage the company, though you could and pay him or her from your DIY Account. You can serve as manager and make most of the business decisions. But you cannot pay yourself for management work—that would constitute self-dealing.

There also might be restrictions on what exactly you can do as an LLC manager. Some legal commentators have suggested you don't want to provide any services beyond management and investment oversight. The IRS requires all contributions to a DIY Account to be made in cash, so if you do other work that increases the company's value—you personally fix up the apartment you're renting out—you might be deemed in violation. Experts recommend avoiding any physical work for the LLC yourself—hire others!

You can add money from your DIY Account periodically into the LLC.[5] Just be sure to keep a good paper trail to show all money moved between the DIY Account and the LLC, with none of it ever touching your personal accounts. One person got into hot water when his non-IRA companies made payments to his IRA LLC.[6] Any comingling of funds between your DIY Account and your own funds is strictly prohibited. If you want to take money out of the company, it must be first transferred to your DIY Account and then from that Account to you through a formal distribution.

Your DIY Account also can join with other DIY Accounts to form a DIY partnership. And multiple investors can cofinance with your Account as well. Once you do so, the LLC has to file a federal partnership tax return each year. Several important rules apply here.

First, it's legally better if the LLC is formed at the outset by the multiple partners, including your Account. There should be clarity about how much money each partner has contributed to get started, with voting power within the LLC allocated accordingly. Later on, we'll talk about why "disqualified" persons—like your kids—cannot own 50 percent or more of the LLC. (If they own less than 50 percent, there are additional rules you need to follow.) If the LLC requires more capital, perhaps to pay special expenses, every partner needs to contribute exactly in proportion to his or her share. Otherwise, your Account might accidentally gain or lose its ownership share vis-à-vis another partner with whom a transfer of money is prohibited.

In theory you personally and your DIY Account can co-own an LLC. *But this is dangerous, if you do even the slightest thing wrong.* Suppose you want to buy a piece of property and don't have enough money personally to make the down payment. Can you form an LLC with your DIY Account and then proceed? No.[7] You cannot create an LLC to "enable" a personal transaction that you couldn't do without your retirement funds.

As you can see, knowing what's permissible and what's not in these situations can be difficult. The line is blurry, depending on the facts. For these types of questions, you'll definitely want to seek the advice of an attorney.

More broadly, if you create an LLC associated with your DIY Account, review *everything* with an attorney. An experienced attorney or accountant can help you prepare all the proper paperwork, including an appropriate articles of incorporation, an appropriate LLC operating agreement, a tax ID with the DIY Account listed as the owner, a subscription agreement outlining the money initially invested, and a "buy direction" letter indicating the funds transferred from the Account to the LLC.

An experienced custodian can help introduce you to the right people as well. Not all custodians, for example, will permit this LLC creation, even though it's perfectly legal. This is the kind of question you will want to ask before hiring your custodian. If you have a Solo 401k, you will want to make sure that your "prototype" agreement permits creating your own LLC.

The Bottom Line

The universe of local investments is small but expanding rapidly. Your mission is to find them. There are simple steps you can take that should unearth all the opportunities you need: analyze your own needs and your kids' needs; approach local businesses, nonprofits, and cooperatives you love; find other interested people in your community; check out what's listed on the crowdfunding websites through Investibule; create a regular meeting space for local businesses and investors (a LION chapter); create a website with local investment opportunities; and start a local investment club.

The fallback option is to invest in yourself by creating your own LLC. You also can create an LLC with other DIY Accounts, other investors, and even your personal funds. Because mistakes here can easily get you into legal hot water, you will want to consult with a good attorney before proceeding.

8

EVALUATING LOCAL
INVESTMENTS

A good local investor must be a good investor in general. You need to learn how to discern your own investment goals, evaluate investment opportunities, and create a good portfolio to manage risk. For the moment, all these tasks will require some work. Until there's a local investment fund or a local-friendly registered investment advisor (RIA) in every backyard, you probably will have to find, evaluate, and select local investments on your own, one by one. And just like learning any skill, like tennis or woodworking, becoming a good local investor requires commitment and practice.

That said, there are ways to make the workload manageable. You might focus on one type of investment to gain expertise in it—perhaps small bond issues from your local government, or local real estate. You might take advantage of the expertise you already have in one field, perhaps in local food businesses or local energy businesses. Or you might put together a local investment club so that you can share with others the work and the fun.

But let's start with you.

How Should You Think about Your Own Local Investment Goals?

Why are you investing locally? To make money for your retirement? To support your community? To enjoy yourself? Some combination of these?

There are two issues you especially should do some hard thinking about—risk and liquidity. How much risk are you willing to tolerate? The entire universe of local investment carries special risk because it's immature. We already talked about some of the risks, such as the risk of not finding enough investment options and choosing the wrong one, or the risk of the entire community entering a recession and tanking your portfolio. To that end, let's add the risk that everyone participating in this universe—you, other local investors, local businesses, local government—is on a steep learning curve.

But that doesn't necessarily mean that continuing to invest in Wall Street carries less risk. To the contrary, there are profound risks that the traditional markets could crash again. And the rise of local investment alternatives will actually increase the riskiness of traditional investments, because as investors move to local securities, the value of traditional stocks and bonds could plunge.

There's risk no matter what you do. When you review any investment document, whether for a local or global deal, it typically warns you—be prepared to lose everything. You'll sign, even though you are not prepared to lose *everything*.

But you do need to ask yourself about your tolerance for loss. How much of your retirement savings are you really prepared to lose next year?

If the answer is "zero"—if you can't afford *any* losses—then perhaps you should consider putting all your money into federal government bonds or bank certificates of deposit. Those are pretty much the lowest-risk securities available. But their rates of return are anemic. If you want to make some money, you will have to take on more risk. But how much? How about putting half your investments in very low-risk securities and half in higher-risk things? Does this feel right? Do you want to risk more still for more reward? Risk less?

Angela Barbash, whom we met in Chapter 7, is one of the few RIAs in the United States who actually helps her clients find local investments. Her company, Revalue, based in Ypsilanti, Michigan, works with clients to integrate local businesses into their portfolios. After the financial meltdown of 2008, Angela's clients were eager to find local alternatives to Wall Street, and she realized that she had no good answers. Local securities were never part of her RIA training or exams. So she went to a Slow Money conference in San Francisco in 2011 and was thrilled to meet other RIAs who were being asked the same questions.

Fast forward eight years and Barbash now is reinventing the entire RIA practice. She's done enough research in her region to identify promising local investment opportunities, some for accredited clients and some for everyone else. She has developed enough discernment that she has not introduced her clients to any local losers. Still, she's careful to make sure her clients look carefully at their own tolerance for risk before investing locally.

She asks her clients to look at risk from three angles. The first is their emotional tolerance for risk. How far would the stock market have to drop, she asks, for you to convert all your investments to cash? Here's a related question: How did you respond when the market did precipitously collapse in 2008? If a small drop spooks you, if you sold everything in 2008, then your tolerance for risk is low. These people, Barbash says, should not do anything that ruins their sleep, their health, and their relationships.

Barbash recommends that highly risk-averse people invest no more than 1 percent in local business. Those with a moderate risk tolerance might invest 5 percent. Those who enjoy higher risk taking could move to 10 percent. She concedes she is only referring to investment in local businesses and community capital funds. The other forms of local investing in yourself, such as getting out of credit card debt or investing in your own home, are low risk and can justify a substantially higher allocation. In fact, Barbash admits that nearly all her own retirement savings are in her house and her business.

Next, Barbash has clients plan out their expected financial needs for the rest of their lives. Most financial advisors divide life into two stages—"accumulation" during your working life and "distribution" during your retired life. Barbash insists on more nuance. When will you need to pay for your kids' college? When do you think you will need a new car? Have you planned for a vacation each year? Do you have at least $20,000 tucked away for emergencies? Do you plan to continue working, but maybe fewer hours, in your seventies? Barbash helps clients map out all their anticipated periods of need through scenario planning and tries to make sure they have all the cash they need in each life stage ahead.

When you're young and you have a lot of investing years ahead of you, you're usually willing to take more risk. If the market suddenly collapses, you have many potentially great market years ahead to make up for the loss. When you're old and nearing retirement and you can't afford a loss, you need to shy away from risk.

The third question—and the most obvious—is your financial needs. Objectively, what can you afford to lose? The wealthier you are, the more you can tolerate risky investments. If you're living from paycheck to paycheck, you need to stick with low-risk options.

It's worth emphasizing again that some local investments are actually low risk. For the low risk part of your portfolio, you might want to focus on getting out of debt and paying off your house. Or you will want to put money into your local bank or municipal bonds. For money you're willing to take more risk with, you might invest in local companies— but only those that have been around for a while and whose products, services, and management you trust. You should only invest in very high-risk companies, like startups, if you're really prepared to lose that money.

Note that the riskiness question is different from whether the investment is supportive of your community. Almost all local investment options will meet that criterion. Whether high or low risk, almost all local investment options boost local jobs, spending, and taxes.

If you're still stumped by how to get started, here's one suggestion in line with Barbash's earlier advice: Begin slowly and cautiously. How about investing 1 percent of your portfolio in local stuff immediately? If you're happy with how you are doing after a year, then add 1 percent more. Then another 1 percent at the end of year two. And so forth.

Implicit in a risk analysis is liquidity. Liquidity represents your ability to turn your investment into cash. No one want to hold ownership certificates or paper bonds forever, especially when your kids are going to college or you face huge medical bills. Putting money on deposit in a bank is almost perfectly liquid, unless you've bought CDs with a certain number of years to mature. Investing in local business is relatively illiquid, because it's hard to find marketplaces where you can resell your stock shares. Other local securities—say, local bonds or local loans—will have fixed dates for their repayments and are somewhat liquid.

Like your tolerance for risk, your need for liquidity will change throughout your life. Earlier in your life, you won't need the funds. As you near and proceed through retirement, you will want to start cashing things in.

Even though the lack of liquidity poses risk, it is also different from risk. Think about certificate deposits at your local bank that fully mature in ten years. These are not liquid but very low risk. Alternatively, you might hold deposits of Russian rubles—a currency that's very liquid but, given the instability of that part of the world, very high risk.

One helpful way to think about these questions is to create a very simple grid with four quadrants. This is a methodology developed by two colleagues of mine: Amy Pearl, who led the campaign to change Oregon's crowdfunding laws, and Marco Vangelisti, a PhD economist and mathematician who was a founding member of Slow Money. Both teach classes with this technique.

Take a look at Chart 7. Put numbers into each quadrant so that all four add up to 100 percent. For example, if you were very risk averse, you might put 5 percent in each of the two "High Risk" boxes, 10 percent in "Low Risk, Low Liquidity," and 80 percent in "Low Risk, High Liquidity." If you were young and adventurous, your highest percentages would go into the "High Risk" boxes.

Chart 7. What Are Your Own Risk and Liquidity Requirements?

	LOW RISK	HIGH RISK
LOW LIQUIDITY	%	%
HIGH LIQUIDITY	%	%

As you make local investment decisions, try to match your choices with this allocation. Chart 8 shows some examples of local investment opportunities for each category.

Chart 8. Examples of Local Investment by Risk and Liquidity

	LOW RISK	HIGH RISK
LOW LIQUIDITY	Investment in Energy Efficiency Long-Term Bank CDs	Stock in a Local Startup Long-Term Loan to a Neighbor
HIGH LIQUIDITY	Municipal Bonds Deposits in a Credit Union Paying Down Credit Cards	Short-Term Loan to a Local Startup Short-Term Loan to a Neighbor

How Should You Evaluate Local Investment Opportunities?

Once you've figured out how you wish to allocate your portfolio in theory, you should assess all your local investment options for their return, risk, and liquidity. You can do this yourself, but it will be better if you join up with friends and neighbors who share your interest in local investing.

Be aware that the information formally presented to you is almost always incomplete. Even a company that has gone through the elaborate process of preparing a direct public offering or a Reg A offering statement will employ dense, inscrutable boilerplate in critical sections. You might find a section, for example, called "risks," where every conceivable risk short of a Martian invasion is listed—and you will still have no real idea which risks are most serious. By law, federally licensed crowdfunding portals cannot share their business judgments about the deals they present. They have a checklist they must go through—board members must not have a shady history, your accounting firm must sign off on your financials, your materials cannot contain any fraudulent promises—but they cannot make any pronouncement like "the chances of this wobbly business surviving another twelve months is slim to none." This means that you will need to do some serious research yourself.

Barbash encourages clients to "find your tribe." Some people who are inherently social like to work in a local group. Others, like engineers, prefer to dig deep into data, and will gravitate toward other engineers in online chat groups. Still others, who Barbash calls professors, will develop national networks and share information about the performance of, say, microbreweries.

Whatever your tribe, you will want to scrutinize each potential local investment and begin the process of "due diligence." Imagine yourself as a banker interviewing a potential loan applicant. If the client were a business, here are some top items you might inquire about:

- *Intuition*—What does your gut say? (Barbash says that if you don't understand the business, it's probably a bad investment. That's Warren Buffett's philosophy as well.)

- *Core Business*—How strong is the core business? Do you love its products or services?

- *Competitors*—How many competitors does the business have locally? How does the business distinguish itself from its peers?

- *Intellectual Property (IP)*—Has the company done enough to protect its IP through patents and trademarks? If the company does not have unique IP, what's the danger of the model being copied?

- *Management*—Is the business under strong leadership? Do you have faith in the promises made to you as an investor? Do you trust the managers?

- *Workforce*—Does the company have a talented, enthusiastic workforce? Are they compensated well, not just with wages but with benefits? Are they loyal to the company? Do they have a role in management? Do they share in ownership?

- *Financials*—Do you have access to the company's recent financials? Its profit-and-loss statements? Its balance sheet? If you don't know much about accounting, you might ask a friend who does to help review these reports.

- *Projections*—Do the company's assertions about its projected growth make sense, given its past performance?

- *Social Performance*—What's the company's environmental record? Social performance? How much does it give to charity? Companies with high social performance tend to be more trustworthy.

- *Exit*—What's the end game for the company? Does it want to thrive locally? Grow into a franchise or chain? Be bought out? How will this affect your return?

You will also want to ask questions about the nature of the investment you're considering:

- *Loans*—If you are being promised a steady payment over a term of years, what happens if a payment is missed? What are your rights then?

- *Stock*—Are dividends being promised? When can you sell the stock? Are there limits on who you can sell the stock to? Will the company buy back stock and, if so, when and at what price?

All these factors will give you a sense of the riskiness of your investment. There's no question that this takes time and is but another reason to share the burden with partners. But the effort will help you develop personal trust in the firm and excitement about it. How many Wall Street companies would allow you to run through these questions with a senior manager? A strong local business prospect will gladly provide you with this information.

If the potential investment involves not a business but an individual, your questions will be a little different. If you were making a loan to a neighbor, you'd want to know about her job, her likely income, her assets, and her reliability. You also might want to ask for collateral. A loan with collateral or some other form of security is a lot less risky than a nonrecourse loan.

With either a business or an individual, you will want to assess the liquidity in the years ahead. Loans, especially those paid back in steady installments over a small number of years, are relatively liquid. The same is true of royalty agreements, which pay you based on revenues or profits over a certain period. Stock certificates, in contrast, usually come with some restrictions on resale. Make sure you understand these before you buy.

How Can You Put Together a Sound Local Investment Portfolio?

Another way to hedge your risk is through a diversified portfolio. A stock's price, for example, can go up or it can go down. Most of us just bet on the price going up. But a savvy and risk-averse investor will make two bets—one on the assumption that the price will go up (investing "long") and the other on the assumption that it will go down (investing "short"). That investor is said to be hedging one bet with the other. And using some pretty wild math, a hedging investor can figure out how to make money either way.

Most investors hedge by diversifying their portfolios. You want a bunch of investments that cover a wide range of possibilities. If one of your investments does poorly because of some unforeseen event, you want your other investments to be unaffected.

This explains why investment advisors might encourage you to diversify your portfolio with stocks and bonds or with "value" and "growth" stocks. Except these kinds of hedges do very little to diversify your holdings, because you are really holding different kinds of securities from the exact same Fortune 500 companies. If there's a national recession—another 9/11, tech meltdown, or mortgage-market implosion—all these companies and all their securities will suffer.

That's one of the unique advantages of local investment. The economy of some communities and some local industries may be unaffected by national events. During the last recession in 2008, some states—like Vermont, Wyoming, and North Dakota—remained largely unaffected and maintained full employment. By gradually replacing some of your global securities with local investments, you can actually achieve greater diversification. Up to a point.

Remember, there's also risk in putting all your eggs in one geographic basket. If something causes your community's economy to plummet—maybe a hurricane hits, or an anchor factory suddenly departs for Vietnam—all the local companies will be adversely affected. The solution, however, is not to shun local companies. Instead, you might want to invest in local companies in several different regions. Or if someone ever creates a fund of investments supporting local food businesses all over the country, that could diversify your holdings as well.

Economists and business professors have done a lot of research on this question, and many believe that even a half-dozen truly different kinds of investment will provide you with enough diversity. You might split your local investment into different buckets—some in real estate, some in local businesses, and some in local student-debt relief.

The Bottom Line

If you want to be a smart local investor, follow these simple rules:

- Be aware of your own tolerance for risk and need for liquidity for the years ahead and pick local investments that match your needs.

- Perform due diligence on all companies, securities, and individuals in your community that you might invest in.

- Make sure your portfolio is diversified by mixing national and local securities, holding different kinds of local investment, or holding local investments from different regions.

9

SCREENING OUT PROHIBITED TRANSACTIONS

The DIY Accounts can open your options for local investment, but there are limits. The IRS has laid out numerous high-voltage wires that you or your custodian must avoid. Like the *Mission Impossible* assignments, listen to these rules carefully and memorize them (before the message self-destructs!):

- You cannot invest in certain family members who are close to you.

- You cannot take actions that benefit yourself or your lineal family, even indirectly.

- You cannot make investments that are especially difficult to value.

- You cannot make investments that appear to be exerting influences beyond making a reasonable return.

The consequences of violating these rules are severe, so it's essential that you understand and follow these rules. That said, I appreciate that the legal dos and don'ts laid out in this chapter might be confusing and generate a severe headache. The bottom line, which I'll get to, is that there are simple rules you can follow to stay far, far away from anything that could possibly get you in trouble.

Who Are "Disqualified" Persons?

The first type of prohibition concerns the person, people, or entity in which you are investing. In IRS lingo, some people or entities are "disqualified" from receiving your investments. You *cannot* invest in[1]

- Yourself;

- Your trustee or custodian;

- Most members of your immediate family, including your spouse, parents, grandparents, children and their spouses;

- A business, a trust, or an estate in which you or your family have a controlling interest;

- A key individual in a business, a trust, or an estate in which you or your family have a controlling interest. This includes a corporation's officer, director, major shareholder (owning 10 percent or more of the outstanding shares), or major wage earner (earning 10 percent or more of the total wages paid).[2]

You not only cannot invest in a disqualified person directly, you cannot benefit them even indirectly. This is a murky area of the law, since it sometimes depends on the facts and circumstances of a situation. But below are a bunch of examples of transactions that the IRS has pronounced as prohibited—and keep in mind that this list is hardly complete. Let's assume you were looking to invest funds from your Solo 401k and considering possible transactions with your son, Jerry. Here's what lawyers expert in the field would likely advise:

- Your Solo 401k cannot sell or lease property to Jerry, nor buy or lease property from him.

- Your Solo 401k cannot buy stock or an LLC interest from Jerry, nor sell these securities to him.

- Your Solo 401k cannot lend Jerry money, nor even guarantee the loan. Your DIY Account also cannot borrow money from him.[3]

- Your Solo 401k cannot sell goods or services to Jerry, nor buy them from him.

- If your Solo 401k owns property, you cannot pay Jerry to cover its upkeep or hire him to manage the property or do repairs.

- Your Solo 401k cannot transfer any income or assets to Jerry.

- If your Solo 401k owns a house, you cannot allow Jerry to rent from you. Nor can you even allow him to stay there *for free*.

- If Jerry were a real estate agent and sold a house owned by your Solo 401k, he could not receive a commission for the sale.

You, of course, are also prohibited from undertaking these activities between your DIY Account and yourself. You cannot sell property to your plan, even at a fair market value, because you are a disqualified person with respect to your plan. You cannot use your Self-Directed IRA to buy a home for yourself and live there.[4] Your Self-Directed IRA cannot loan money to yourself (though you could use your Solo 401k).[5] And you cannot add any personal money or a guarantee for your Self-Directed IRA to buy property or a business.[6]

Your DIY Account can obtain a loan to buy property, but you cannot put your Account on the line for any shortfall. That means you have to find a bank that provides your Account with a nonrecourse loan, which in the event of a default only allows the bank to take back the property. Unlike other kinds of loans, a nonrecourse loan is not based on your personal credit history, personal assets, or personal guarantees. Moreover, as explained in the next section, under the self-dealing rules, you cannot personally add funds or personally guarantee this transaction—it must remain completely between your DIY Account and the bank.

Some lenders specialize in providing nonrecourse loans and they tend to look, at least when it comes to a loan for real estate, for two things:[7] The property should be producing rental income for your DIY Account, and your Account should be prepared to pay as much as 30 to 40 percent of the equity in a down payment. But beware a common mistake: Some lenders present you with documents to sign in which you personally guarantee against fraud or misappropriation of funds. This is impermissible. Your personal guarantee amounts to comingling your money with your Account's. Have an attorney review this language before you sign.

You may have noticed who's not on the list of disqualified persons. The IRS is only concerned with direct lineal descendants or ancestors. You can freely engage in transactions with brothers, sisters, step siblings, aunts, uncles, and cousins. You're also welcome to do transactions with friends, as well as coworkers, neighbors, and strangers.

Perhaps the most confusing and difficult disqualified person is a business in which you have a "controlling interest."[8] It generally means the disqualified person cannot own 50 percent or more of the company. If, say, your family owns 49 percent or less of the company, your Solo 401k can invest in or otherwise do business with it. But the meaning of controlling interest varies, depending on the type of entity:

- A *corporation* is disqualified if your family controls 50 percent or more of the voting stock.

- A *partnership* is disqualified if your family receives 50 percent or more of the profits or capital interest.

- A *trust* or an *unincorporated business entity* is disqualified if your family has 50 percent or more of the beneficial interest.

And then there's the matter of an LLC. We earlier noted that a Self-Directed IRA could create an LLC. This might seem like a contradiction with the control requirement, but the law is a funny thing. An LLC is considered an extension of the creator, and in this case your Account is the creator, not you. This is not the case for a separate entity like a corporation, partnership, or trust.

There's also a difference between your DIY Account creating an LLC or buying an existing LLC, which is acceptable, and your Account buying a share of an LLC you already own personally. The act of your Account buying an interest in your personal business—an act in which you are both the buyer and seller—creates problems.

There's also a problem with your Account entering into transactions with key individuals in the companies where your family has a controlling interest. Anyone with significant power in a company you or your family personally controls is off limits for your Account. This includes any officer, director, or board member involved in the company. It also includes any individual who owns 10 percent or more of the enterprise. And it includes any highly compensated employee, which is defined as someone who receives 10 percent or more of a company's wages.

What Constitutes Self-Dealing?

One of the trickiest rules to understand is that you or another disqualified person cannot *indirectly* benefit in any way from your DIY Account. This explains why, if your Account owns property, you or your family cannot even stay there one night for free.

If you decide to invest in a local ice cream company, you can continue to buy ice cream there. But if special discounts are offered to shareholders, you cannot take advantage of them personally. And if your DIY Account bought the whole ice cream company, you couldn't give yourself and your kids special access to free samples.

This concept is inherently confusing. After all, isn't the whole purpose of your opening a DIY Investment Account to benefit you? Yes, but *only when you begin making withdrawals*. Until that point, your personal finances and financial interests need to be separated clearly from those of your Self-Directed IRA or Solo 401k. That's the nature of a trust.

Let's look at that example where you might stay in a property owned by your DIY Account. If you pay the same rent as everyone else, shouldn't that be okay? Your stay would no longer be self-dealing, but it would still be a prohibited transaction. Remember, your Account cannot enter into any contract—including a rental arrangement—with any disqualified person, including yourself.

Here are some other examples of self-dealing drawn from cutting-edge law cases:

- Your Account, in some circumstances, cannot invest in a company where you are a partner holding a minority stake.[9]

- Your Account cannot invest in a property with an expectation that you will receive a contract or special compensation from the property owner.[10]

- Your Account cannot buy up one of your personal debt notes.[11]

- Your Account cannot buy a high school, founded by your daughter, and lease it back.[12]

- Your law firm's Account cannot lend money to clients awaiting settlement.[13]

These fact patterns, of course, do not provide perfect guidance for every scenario. And there are some areas where the legal cases offer contradictory guidance. An example is the question of whether your Account can provide a loan to a company where you are a partial owner but do not hold a controlling (greater than 50 percent) stake. In *Rollins v. Commissioner*, the

Account holders held noncontrolling stakes but were none-theless the largest owners of the companies borrowing from their Accounts.[14] Their significant influence was enough to convince the tax court that this was self-dealing. But other cases have reached different conclusions.[15]

Experts suggest you need to be especially careful if you are an owner or officer in the company your Account is transacting with. The greater your decision-making influence in the company, the more likely the arrangement will be held to be self-dealing. Here are some other guidelines that might help:

- The more you can influence both sides of the transaction, as was the case in *Rollins*, the more likely you will be found to be self-dealing.

- If you can show that the terms of the transaction were identical to those enjoyed by others, then it's less likely you will be found to be self-dealing.

- The greater your ownership or control in an entity, the more vulnerable you are to be found to be self-dealing. Owning 49 percent of a company, while not a controlling interest, may nonetheless indicate you have undue influence.

You're probably wondering why giving yourself a loan from your Solo 401k isn't self-dealing. It actually is but it's legal because Congress explicitly permits it. Think of it as an exception to the rules. If you want to do anything with your DIY savings to benefit yourself now, best to do it through a loan to yourself. But you can do this only with a Solo 401k, not a Self-Directed IRA, and only if your Solo 401k "proto-type" specifically permits such loans.

There are a bunch of Congressionally created exceptions like this where the transaction seems like self-dealing but is permissible. The relevant statute contains twenty-three exceptions.[16] Here are some other examples:

- If a bank is a fiduciary for your DIY Account, you can deposit some of your funds in an interest-bearing account there.

- If your plan has been issued by an insurance company, you can still buy your own insurance from it.

- You can take a loan from your DIY Account to buy an interest in an employee stock ownership plan.

- A disqualified person can provide your plan with "necessary" services, including office space, accounting, and legal assistance, as long as the compensation is reasonable.

The last exemption is dangerous, though. Suppose you wanted to hire your son, who's an accountant, to manage your plan for a fee. You could do so, but the burden ultimately rests on you to prove to the IRS that the service was "necessary" and the compensation "reasonable."

What's a Categorically Prohibited Investment?

While the IRS allows a huge range of potential investments with your DIY Account, several things are categorically off limits. Three in particular are worth mentioning: stock in S Corporations, collectibles, and life insurance contracts.

Buying S Corporation stock is forbidden.[17] An S Corporation is an election a C Corporation can make to pass all the gains (or losses) directly onto the shareholders. The advantage is that the company's shareholders avoid double taxation (taxation of the corporation, and then taxation of shareholder dividends and stock appreciation). One of the requirements of an S Corporation is that its shareholders cannot include certain trusts, including those overseeing DIY Accounts.

Investing in collectibles is forbidden because the IRS worries about your putting money into items for which it is hard to ascertain fair market value.[18] Among the things that fall into this category are stamps, coins, antiques, baseball cards, horses, gems, bottles of wine, and works of art. The IRS does, however, offer an exception for certain government-approved coins and bullion made from precious metals like gold, silver, platinum, and palladium.

Life insurance contracts constitute one the few areas where the rules for Self-Directed IRAs differ from those for Solo 401ks.[19] A Self-Directed IRA cannot be used to purchase your life insurance under any circumstances, but a Solo 401k can be if several conditions are observed. The plan has to pay income taxes on the insurance protection. If you die while the plan is still in effect, the death benefits come directly to your plan, not your estate. Hopefully, your plan has good instructions about where your money goes after you die!

Are There Any Other Prohibited Transactions?

Yes. And this section can only summarize them. But I encourage you to read Matt Sorensen's *Self Directed IRA Handbook* for additional details.[20] He outlines three additional rules that you need to be mindful of:

- The *Exclusive Benefit Rule* prohibits you from denying your DIY Account a reasonable rate of return.[21] If you make a loan to your sister (who is not a disqualified person) but it's at 1 percent, way below the market rate for loans, you are violating this rule. If you buy a piece of land, and the legal work required for the transaction exceeds the value of the land, that's also a violation. In other words, as a trustee for your DIY Account, you must exercise prudence. Close scrutiny will especially be paid if you make sweetheart deals with people around you, even if they are not disqualified.

- The *Step Transaction Doctrine* essentially says that you cannot circumvent the rules by adding an additional step to a transaction.[22] For example, you cannot make a loan to a stranger and condition it on his making a loan to your son, who's a disqualified person. The initial transaction would be regarded as an invalid "straw person."

- The *Plan Asset Rule* means that when your DIY Account invests in a company, that company—not just your Account—may have to follow all the rules laid out in this chapter.[23] A simple example is if your Account bought an investment company, that company would have to follow the rules and not make loans to you, your kids, or your other companies—all of whom are disqualified recipients of your investment. Even if you held a smaller interest in this company, the Plan Asset Rule might kick in.

Since the Plan Asset Rule is pretty complicated, let's look at it in a little more detail. The magic threshold triggering scrutiny is 25 percent. If retirement plans—and not just yours—collectively own 25 percent or more of a company, the rule kicks in. If a general partner in a hedge fund, for example, has a Solo 401k that owns 26 percent of the fund, that partner becomes disqualified from receiving management fees associated with the Solo 401k. The same consequences would follow if two Accounts owned by general partners each held, say, 13 percent of the fund, because together they would exceed the 25 percent threshold.

This rule is largely about regulating the activities of certain kinds of privately held finance and insurance companies. Companies that produce goods and services are exempt. Real estate companies are exempt. Publicly traded companies are exempt. Even some kinds of finance companies, such as venture capital firms, are exempt. Also, if your DIY Account has just lent the company money and does not have an equity interest, that's also fine.

But, there's an exemption to the exemptions! If your DIY Account owns 100 percent of a given company—any company—the Plan Asset Rule applies. In this case, even the subsidiaries of that company are swept into the restrictions. A subsidiary thus could not provide a loan to any of the DIY plans. Nor could the subsidiary pay any of the DIY plan owners a salary.

The good news is that if you're rich enough to be at risk from these rules, you probably can afford a good attorney to vet them.

What Are the Penalties for Violating These Rules?

Severe!

If an Account owner carries out a prohibited transaction, the IRS may disqualify everything inside the Account. If you discover that a transaction is prohibited, you must fix it immediately. If you don't correct everything within that tax year, the IRS might sack you with an additional penalty of 100 percent of the total investment. And just to show you that it really means business, the IRS can impose these penalties not only on your Account but *also* on the disqualified persons linked with the transaction.

Suppose you violate a rule with, say, an impermissible $20 contract. Your $1 million Account could be completely invalidated. And then you'd have to pay a $100,000 penalty for premature withdrawal (the 10 percent penalty) plus income taxes on the $900,000 distributed. Chances are, moreover, that this new income would put you in a significantly higher tax bracket!

If you are innocent, if the mistake was made by your Self-Directed IRA custodian, for example, the IRS still can impose an excise tax of 15 percent of the total investment *for each year of the transaction*. If you're lucky, the penalty will be imposed on your hapless custodian. Additional penalties might apply unless you correct the mistake immediately—up to 100 percent of the amount involved.

The exact penalty depends on the details. If you were older than fifty-nine and a half when the violation occurred, old enough to take a withdrawal, you wouldn't have to pay the 10 percent penalty but you still would have to pay other taxes.

If you have a Roth Account and are over fifty-nine-and-a-half years old and if the funds were held for at least five years, there would be no additional taxes or penalties. If either of the above conditions were not true, if you were younger than fifty-nine and a half or your contributions were made less than five years ago, you would have to pay taxes on your gains. You don't need to pay taxes on your contributions again. If you were younger than fifty-nine and a half at the time of the violation, you would have to pay the 10 percent penalty for premature withdrawals only if your funds were held for less than five years. Any funds held for more than five years would not be subject to this penalty.

You also can be vulnerable to accuracy-related penalties. The IRS is allowed to assess an additional 20 percent penalty on any substantial underreporting of taxes when there is negligence. If you rely on the advice of a financial professional or an attorney, however, you usually can dodge this bullet.

The only good news is this: If you go awry with one of your DIY Accounts, all your other accounts are unaffected.

The Bottom Line

If you are afraid of these prohibitions and penalties, make sure you stay far, far away from even the gray zones. Absent advice from an attorney, you should probably observe these rules:

- Don't invest in anything that touches you or your lineal family, period.

- Don't invest in any entity run or controlled by you or your lineal family (though an LLC created and controlled by your Account is okay).

- Don't allow yourself or your lineal family to benefit even indirectly from any of your transactions.

- Don't invest in S Corporations, collectibles, or life insurance policies.

- Make sure your transactions are sound, defensible investments, especially if you're investing in anyone in your immediate universe.

- If you are investing in a finance or insurance company, try to avoid any situation where other retirement plans plus yours own more than 25 percent of it.

- The most important rule is this: If you want to cross into any gray zone, be sure to consult a very good attorney or tax consultant first.

10

ADMINISTERING YOUR DIY ACCOUNT

Once you decide how to invest your DIY Account, you need to formalize the transactions with some paperwork. You need to do periodic reporting. You must be mindful that you might owe taxes on unrelated business income. And ultimately, you'll want to start withdrawing funds. None of these tasks are particularly difficult, and that's why this chapter will be short!

How Do You Formalize Your Investment Decisions?

Let's start with a Self-Directed IRA. One of the reasons for having a "custodian" is that this is a person who knows—or should know—how to do most of your legal paperwork. These are the services you're paying her a fee for. Her responsibility is to make sure your investment decisions follow the law.

When you sign up with a custodian, she will probably introduce you to the procedures for making investment choices, which vary from company to company. Generally, you will submit a "Direction of Investment" form to your custodian with the basic information, along with the paperwork appropriate for the given investment (stock, real estate, an LLC, a loan, etc.). The custodian then will review the documents, make sure the proposed transaction is legal, and carry out your instructions. It's possible she may have a few follow-up questions via email or a phone call—but that's it.

Remember that some custodians charge more for complex transactions, such as land deals (because market valuations can be difficult) or LLCs (because they need to create a new business entity). That's why it's helpful to make an intelligent guess about how you will use your DIY Account and shop for a custodian accordingly.

On a rare occasion your custodian may pronounce your local investment illegal or improper even when you are convinced otherwise. Perhaps you're in one of the gray zones we discussed. The solution is to hire an attorney to review the proposed transaction, and if he thinks it's legal, he can try to convince your custodian.

Common problems include these: Your custodian decides the transaction is beyond your original agreement for services. Or beyond her competency (perhaps you're proposing to invest in another country). Or your custodian requires you to prepare some documents first and you haven't. Again, before you hire a custodian, think carefully about the kinds of transactions you are likely to want.

If your custodian is consistently resisting your requests, you're convinced your proposed investments are legal, and your lawyer is having no luck persuading her otherwise, the solution is simple: Time to hire a new custodian who is more comfortable with the transactions you propose.

For a Solo 401k, the paperwork is simple: You write a check and keep track—that's it! But before you write an investment check, you want to be 110 percent confident that the transaction is permissible under your "prototype" and the law. If you're not sure, raise the question within The Next Egg or in your investment club, and others will happily help you out. Some Solo 401k plans also allow you a certain amount of attorney time if you have serious questions.

As is the case for Self-Directed IRAs, you may need to prepare agreements for various kinds of transactions, though local businesses looking for investment typically have these documents. My general philosophy for legal documents is to keep them as basic as possible, using plain language. If you look at the various books written about DIY Accounts listed as references and search around the web, you will find plenty of model agreements that will cost you nothing. Other good sources of low-cost legal forms are the DIY books published by Nolo Press.

You'll want to establish a clear paper trail for all your transactions, making sure that the signatory on all documents is not you personally but you as the trustee of your Solo 401k. If your Account has made a loan, be absolutely sure that the repayments are coming to the Account, not you personally. Keep a good ledger of the checks, and maybe a spreadsheet on your returns.

A Workplace DIY Plan in Colorado

Jason Wiener, thirty-nine, represents a new breed of mission-oriented attorneys. His six-attorney firm has three of counsel and three full-time lawyers located in Colorado and Massachusetts, with clients in thirty states. The practice focuses on promoting "shared ownership" models of business and alternative capital formation.

I met Jason in 2017 at a Regenerative Future Summit, which was held in Boulder where he lives and where I had spoken about local investment. He was inspired to set up a Self-Directed IRA but found it difficult to find the right custodian with affordable fees. He wound up creating a DIY Account at Charles Schwab but felt a "sense of defeat."

A year later, however, he discovered a local company, Qualified Pension Services (QPS), that expertly helped him set up a Solo 401k. The rates were reasonable and the paperwork minimal. They walked him through all his questions about his plan document. It took a little work to find a bank that felt comfortable creating an account in the name of Jason's Solo 401k trust, but he found a nearby employee-owned bank that was willing to proceed.

Right away, Jason put $10,000 into local investment opportunities. Even though he considers himself "very risk tolerant," he had difficulty finding deals where unaccredited investors could participate. What he has found and invested in thus far includes the Clean Energy Federal Credit Union, an investment cooperative called the Kachuwa Fund, and an index of employee-owned companies on a crowdfunding platform called Motif. He's also now looking at the Iroquois Valley Fund, which is helping to protect farmland, and the Ujima Fund in Boston, which supports local entrepreneurs of color. To make the workload of reviewing these investments manageable, he also joined a local investment club.

Jason regards his Solo 401k as a stepping stone to something bigger—a full-fledged, employer sponsored, partially self-directed 401k program. Working closely with QPS, he has set up a workplace plan that his employees can opt into. Jason manages the portfolio but consults regularly with his colleagues before making local investments. He crafted an investment policy that is tailored to a portfolio of traditional Vanguard investments as well as self-directed investments. Jason works with participating employees to source, undertake due diligence for, and recommend investments with up to 25–30 percent of an employee's pretax deferrals eligible for such self-directed investments, like the ones Jason made from his Solo 401k.

If your company is interested in setting up a plan like this, Jason offers three pieces of advice: Make sure your employees have the requisite level of sophistication and trust in your judgment. Identify your pipeline of deals before you set up the account. Be especially mindful about maintaining enough liquidity in the account to stay compliant with workplace pension rules.

What Forms Need to Be Filed with the Government?

Very few.

For the Self-Directed IRA, most of the paperwork for the ongoing operation of the Account is handled by your custodian. On your individual tax returns, you will report contributions and distributions. That's all, unless you face special taxes called UBITs and UDFIs (discussed shortly), and there are some custodians who will handle the paperwork for these as well.

For a Solo 401k, very little paperwork is required once you adopt a "prototype" plan. Every five or six years, the IRS requires that all plan documents be updated and resubmitted for review. If you subscribe to a Solo 401k plan, your provider will take care of this. Everything else—contributions, distributions, special taxes—is handled exactly as you would handle a Self-Directed IRA, only you are responsible, not a custodian.

Large Solo 401ks have one additional filing requirement. If by the end of the previous tax year your Account is worth more than $250,000, you need to file a short information form (Form 5500-EZ, due the following July 31st).

If your Account owns a company, then you will have to file—on behalf of your Account—the appropriate corporate tax form, depending on the type of company. Except for LLCs: If your Account owns an LLC, you do not have to file anything.

What the Heck Are UBITs and UDFIs?

Not flying saucers, but something more ominous and alien—taxes. Generally, the gains from your DIY Account investments are tax free. But there are two circumstances where your Account may have to pay some taxes. Unrelated Business Income Taxes (UBITs) come into play when your income is not generated "passively." Taxes on Unrelated Debt-Financed Income (UDFI) might be triggered if you are leveraging outside debt to increase your gains. Both are a bit complicated.

Let's start with the Unrelated Business Income Tax (UBIT). Suppose your DIY Account owns a restaurant that is structured as an S Corporation, where the gains and losses are reported on K-1 forms. If the restaurant were structured as a C Corporation, you might receive dividends or appreciation from resale of your stock—all *passive* gains. Before the dividends were paid, the restaurant would pay corporate taxes on the *active* gains from the business itself. But in an S Corporation or another flow-through entity like an LLC or a partnership, the gains (or losses) come straight to you. The taxes still need to be paid.

The UBIT starts at 15 percent but escalates quickly to 39.6 percent once more than $12,500 is earned. So it requires some planning. The good news is that there are a bunch of exemptions. UBITs do not apply to income from interest, dividends, royalties, rents, and capital gains—these are all regarded as passive income. But if your Account has an LLC that is generating a steady stream of income from the sale of goods or services, your Account will have to pay annual UBIT on that income. And you will need to report this on Form 990-T.

UBITs also can arise with real estate transactions. Normally capital gains earned by your DIY Account are not taxed, but there's an exception for real estate purchased and then sold immediately—what's often called "flipping." Gains from real estate flips are subject to the UBIT.

Drawing the line between a long-term property developer and a short-term flipper is not easy. The lead cases suggest there are four important tests.[1] UBITs are more likely to be assessed if

- You intend to sell property immediately after buying it.

- You hold the property for less than a year.

- You're not involved in a long-term property-development project, which typically involves construction and improvements.

- You flip more than one or two properties during a year.

Again, if your Account gains income from flipping, you will need to pay taxes on it and file Form 990-T. You cannot pay these taxes personally. Form 990-T must be filed on behalf of the DIY Account, and the taxes must be paid out of your Account. But you need to file only if you have more than $1,000 of gross income that would be taxable. Incidental income does not need to be reported. If you think you might face significant UBIT, you might want to consult with attorneys and accountants to strategize ways to minimize your liability.[2]

Unrelated Debt-Financed Income, or UDFI, tax is really just a special type of UBIT that applies to debt-financed property. And it applies only to Self-Directed IRAs, not Solo 401ks. All 401k plans are exempt from this tax!

You'll recall that a DIY Account must use a nonrecourse loan for purchases of real estate. The portion of the ordinary income from the property derived, not from your Account's investment, but from the leveraged debt, is taxable. Debt your DIY uses to acquire a property can trigger a UDFI tax. So can debt to improve the property, if the improvements were reasonably foreseeable upon purchase. So can debt to take cash out of the property's equity.

Most Self-Directed IRAs that obtain real estate through leveraged debt can take big deductions for expenses and depreciation and never need to worry about the UDFI. But if your property has appreciated considerably, you might owe UDFI tax upon sale. To avoid this tax, legal experts make two suggestions. First, avoid debt altogether—just buy real estate outright without using any loans. Second, if you must use debt, be sure to pay it off before you sell the property and then your UDFI liability upon sale will be zero.

How Can You Take a Distribution?

Ultimately, you've saved all your life for a payday. How, then, should you start withdrawing funds from your DIY Accounts when you reach the magical age of retirement?

With your Self-Directed IRA, you *can* start withdrawing funds at age fifty-nine and a half but you *must* begin withdrawing funds at seventy and a half. Earlier, we introduced the concept of the required minimum distribution (RMD). The IRS publishes tables that let you know the exact amount.[3] If you are seventy-six and have $100,000 in your account, your RMD would be $4,545. If you were eighty-six, it would be $7,092. If you were ninety-six, it would be $11,627. As you get older, you must withdraw each year a higher and higher percentage of your savings.

If you have several IRA accounts, you are allowed to take the RMD from just one account to cover the rest, which is especially useful if some of your savings are not very liquid. Whatever the level of distribution, you must pay tax on it. If you fail to take the RMD, the IRS might impose a 50 percent excise tax on the amount not properly distributed.

If your Self-Directed IRA is a Roth, you can begin withdrawing at fifty-nine and a half and there is no RMD. Unlike a regular IRA, there's also no age limit for making new contributions. This flexibility explains why a growing number of people convert some or all of their IRAs into Roth IRAs before they reach the age of fifty-nine and a half. But remember that at the moment of Roth conversion, you must pay taxes on the entire amount converted.

For Solo 401ks, the rules are almost the same. Your prototype will indicate the age of retirement (usually between fifty-nine and a half and sixty-five). The fate of your plan also rests on the fate of your self-employment business. If you shut that business down before you reach retirement age, your prototype hopefully will spell out options for rolling over your savings into another DIY Account. You might, for example, choose to roll your funds into a Roth IRA to avoid an RMD.

If you have to take a distribution, it must come from your Solo 401k. You can't take assets from other Accounts to satisfy your RMD. But don't forget that with a Solo 401k you also can take a short-term distribution (up to five years) by making yourself a loan.

The same considerations that govern your strategies for investing, discussed in Chapter 9, will determine your strategies for disinvesting. Registered investment advisors will advise you to keep as much money in your accounts for as long as you can. But given the RMD requirements, as you get older you will want to ensure that more and more of your portfolio assets are liquid. If you're stuck with one or two big illiquid assets, like ownership rights in a shopping center, there are strategies for divesting yourself in small pieces each year that can meet the RMD requirements. But you probably will need to hire an attorney to structure these properly.

Besides retirement, other "triggering events" might allow you to access without penalties your DIY Accounts sooner, including death, disability, court orders (from divorce, for example), unemployment, and financial hardship. The IRS sees "hardship" in events commonly viewed as emergencies. These can include extraordinary medical expenses not covered by insurance, payments to prevent eviction from a rental unit, and repairs after natural disasters. There are a few other intriguing circumstances that can qualify too, including costs related to the purchase of your principal residence or a year of tuition and room and board expenses for a member of your family.

The IRS expects you to crack open your DIY Accounts only for emergencies if you've already tapped all available assets. These include your and your spouse's assets, insurance monies, loans from your Accounts, and other borrowing.

If you do take a hardship distribution, you will still have to pay tax on it (unless it's a Roth Account)—just not the penalty. You then are prohibited from making any new contributions to any of your Accounts for six months.

One final note. Once you reach the age of retirement, you *can* withdraw all your funds in a lump sum if you want. But remember that you will have to pay taxes on all the funds taken out, and a lump sum withdrawal might throw you into a higher tax bracket. It's smarter to spread out your withdrawals, which lowers your annual income and your annual taxes. You can then take payments quarterly, monthly, or irregularly.

The Bottom Line

The administration of the DIY Accounts is relatively simple. You just report contributions and distributions on your individual taxes. If you have a Self-Directed IRA, your custodian will do the rest. If you have a Solo 401k, you need to create a good paper trail of all your transactions, but you have to file a special form with the IRS only if your account has more than $250,000.

Distributing your assets once you pass the age of retirement is relatively easy, as long as you meet your minimum required distributions. The harder part is figuring out your financial needs in retirement and planning your distributions accordingly. And making all the right local investments when you're younger!

11

PREPARING FOR THE FUTURE

Saddle up! We are all pioneers venturing into unmapped territories. "It's tough to make predictions," Yogi Berra once said, "especially about the future." But here's one prediction I can make with confidence: Local investment opportunities will very soon become easier to find, evaluate, and transact. And some of them will become more lucrative. We are at the beginning of what historians might someday call the Great Local Investment Revolution.

Come On, What's So Revolutionary about Money?

Everything!

By the time this book is published, US citizens probably will have invested nearly a billion dollars locally since 2016 through investment crowdfunding. That's a tiny sliver of the $85 trillion dollars in financial assets Americans have, but it's a start.

As more people in your community invest locally, more local businesses will get financed, more municipal infrastructure will be built, more of your neighbors will become homeowners, and more of those struggling with crushing debt will find a way out. As more investors begin to localize their portfolios, they will expand local income, wealth, and jobs, which in turn will enlarge the tax base, gin up public services, and improve the quality of local life. This could be the holy grail of economic development that so many communities have been searching for, far more reliable and cost-effective than giving away billions of dollars of "incentives" to attract and retain global businesses like Amazon.

There also will be losers. As competitive local businesses get more capital, big companies will experience a decapitalization—some dramatically so. What happens when the first trillion dollars moves from Wall Street to Main Street? As demand shifts, the price of Wall Street stocks will drop and the price of Main Street stocks will go up. As more mainstream investors start to notice that the smart money is moving into local business, they too will join in. So will investment advisors. This trend will accelerate until local businesses receive the 60–80 percent of available capital they deserve. And the shift could be stunningly swift.

Among the first major companies to decapitalize may be the "too big to fail" banks, investment houses, brokerages, and other institutions responsible for the crisis of 2008. Were it not for the massive government bailout in the years that followed—not just the $700-billion-dollar relief package that Congress passed in 2008, but the trillions more pumped into the economy by the Federal Reserve through "quantitative easement"—many of these financial behemoths would have gone extinct. If these companies continue to cater exclusively to global finance, their volume of business will steadily shrink. And their competitors at the local level—credit unions, local financial advisors, local investment funds—will multiply. The nation's financial system will become more diverse, safe, and stable.

There are four pillars of the emerging local investment ecosystem:

- *Issuing*—Local businesses will be able to issue securities to grassroots investors more easily and inexpensively.

- *Reselling*—Local stock markets or other "intermediaries" will become available for the purchasers of local securities to resell them, whenever they want, locally. This will help prevent local investors from getting stuck holding worthless pieces of paper.

- *Pooling*—Local investment funds will become more widespread, making it easier for local investors to put their money into diversified pools of capital. Experienced managers running these pools will relieve local investors of the burden of evaluating all the companies, projects, or people they put their money into.

- *Institutionalizing*—Local mutual funds will be set up to help big institutional investors like hospitals, churches, and labor unions put their money into appropriate local investment funds and securities.

What is not widely appreciated, however, is how much each pillar depends on the others. Mutual funds will probably never become seriously interested in local investment until they can see many local investment pools operating with good track records. Local investment funds will never get very far until there are local exchanges or intermediaries where they can sell their securities from time to time. And local exchanges will never be formed until there is a critical mass of local investors looking to use them.

Right now, the local investment ecosystem is filled with a bunch of fragile seedlings. With the JOBS Act and state securities reforms, we have made it easier for local businesses to sell securities—but that's about it. No state has created its own local stock market, though Michigan passed a symbolic law to explore the idea. About two dozen local investment funds across the country allow grassroots investors to participate. Nearly all of them take advantage of the exemption in the Investment Company Act for nonprofits. To really expand the number of these funds, we need new kinds of funds that take advantage of the more than a dozen other exemptions in the Act.[1]

The home-run reform, which conservatives would surely rally around, can be summarized in one word: Federalism! We should allow states to experiment with new local investment frameworks and institutions. While federal laws permit states to frame their own laws about issuing local securities, they do not clearly give the states authority to create local stock markets or local investment funds. They should. States should become "laboratories of democracy" when it comes to investing. Congress might consider passing a very short law allowing this, but there's no reason to wait: The SEC has all the authority it needs to issue a "no action letter" saying that whatever states do regarding their own investors and intrastate securities is their own business—period.

Once this very modest policy declaration occurs, US states will be happily surprised to find plenty of models around the world that they might adopt. In 1999, the Canadian province of Nova Scotia passed a law permitting grassroots groups to set up local investment funds inexpensively, and more than sixty funds have been created since. If the United States had as many funds per capita, we would have 21,000! It shows the importance of getting the law right. In the Canadian province of Alberta, with vast oil resources that make it the Texas of the north, co-ops are given special privileges to become investment funds to stimulate local economic development.

It's harder to find examples around the world of local stock exchanges, except in our own history. In the late 1800s and early 1900s dozens of small stock exchanges scattered across the United States facilitated the buying and selling of shares of local companies. They were indispensable tools for regional economic development. We need to bring these exchanges back. Every state should have at least one virtual exchange where residents can find local companies. If I live in Montana, I should be able to sign up for the Big Sky Exchange, search for "organic food" companies, and quickly find fifty interesting places to park my money. Unlike today's two principal exchanges operating in the United States, the New York Stock Exchange and the NASDAQ, these local exchanges might maintain higher standards of social responsibility and favor slower transactions that discourage speculation.

All this will take time. If you're like me, however, you may be impatient. The gap between rich and poor is yawning. The legions of homeless on our streets are expanding. Traditional jobs are under threat from cheap labor abroad and robots at home. The climate is getting hotter, and water supplies are dwindling. We have got to act now.

What Can Be Done Immediately?

The faster law and policy change, the more local investment options you will have, and the more likely it is that you will find the right ones that fit with your needs for return, risk, and liquidity. We can accelerate this process by bringing down the costs of local investing. While there are a zillion things the federal government can do, I'm going to focus on where we have more influence—state and local governments.

The spread of Self-Directed IRAs and Solo 401ks can greatly increase the number of local investors and the amount of money they move from Wall Street to Main Street. DIY Accounts cost something—not a lot, but something—and like speed bumps, their fees slow down the local investment revolution. Suppose we could bring down those costs. Automation and competition are likely to do this anyway, and I predict that the cost of a Self-Directed IRA and Solo 401k will ultimately shrink to about $100–200 per year, maybe even less. But let's go further and get rid of these costs altogether.

One way to do this effectively might be through a local investment tax credit. For every dollar you put into local investment, you might get some amount off on your taxes. Suppose you had a 5 percent state tax credit. If you reinvested $10,000 of your DIY Account into local business, you would get a $500 credit on your state income or property taxes—more than enough to cover your fees for a year. Better still, let's apply the credit to the total amount of local investments you hold, so you can apply it year after year.

Tax credits exist in many states for a variety of purposes, but none are designed to facilitate local investing by unaccredited investors. A great example can be found just above the US border. The province of New Brunswick, which abuts the state of Maine, recently passed a tax credit to promote local investment. Residents there get fifty cents off every dollar they pay in provincial taxes. There's no reason US states couldn't pass a tax credit like New Brunswick's. In fact, several state legislators are already drafting pieces of legislation to do this. How about yours?

What else should we ask policymakers to do? Let's start with your city council. You might kindly request they consider the following:

- Create a local property tax credit for local investments.

- Move the city's banking into a local bank or credit union, as the cities of Phoenix and Tucson have done. This boosts local financial institutions and keeps more money recirculating at home.

- Publish a list of every local investment opportunity on the city's official website. This would be just for informational purposes, but it could help investors and businesses find one another for private deal-making.

- Encourage your city to issue municipal bonds for important local projects like expanding local renewable-energy capacity, and make it possible for grassroots investors to buy those bonds.

- Create a local land trust with both public and philanthropic funds that can buy up residential land for

affordable housing and commercial land for affordable retail development. Allow grassroots investors to
add capital as well.

- Share with businesses innovative structures that law
firms like Jason Wiener's are using to provide their
employees with self-direction options.

- Start economic-development funds that are run by
the city but capitalized by grassroots investors (this
is an exemption in the Investment Company Act that
has yet to be exploited). Such pools might focus on
food startups or affordable housing. Or they might
help early-stage entrepreneurs find funds to pay for
otherwise steep zoning and licensing fees.

- Get the managers of the city's public employee pension funds to start putting money into local investment options—perhaps through municipal bonds or
land trust loans mentioned previously. They could
provide their employees with DIY options.

Please don't stop there. Get busy at your statehouse too.
After your state legislators pass a local investment tax credit,
you might ask them to try these ideas:

- State leaders should formally ask the Securities and
Exchange Commission for the "no action letter" just
discussed—that is, *permission* for creative financial
entrepreneurs within the state to begin experiment-
ing with local stock exchanges and local investment
funds. Once that permission is granted, experiment
away! Create a local stock market. Make it easy for
local investment funds to get established. Create

simple tests for knowledgeable residents who are not rich to qualify as accredited investors.

- Create a new state agency that evaluates local business securities and makes that information available to investors. Sooner or later, this will probably be done privately—as Moody's or Standard & Poor's do for big companies—but we need some early models to get things moving.

- Check what your state has done with crowdfunding. Is your state one of the dozen, like California or New York, that hasn't legalized it yet? Even in states that do allow local crowdfunding, much more is possible. Raise the limits on the amount a company can raise ($10–20 million seems right) and the amount unaccredited investors presumptively can give (some states allow up to $10,000 per year). Sound the rams' horns to break down the Jericho-like walls that keep grassroots money away from local businesses.

- States have impeded intrastate crowdfunding through their rules governing "community portals," where local investors and businesses do transactions in a legally compliant way. The SEC now allows portals licensed under the JOBS Act to be run by anyone and these portals can charge a success fee, which pays the bills and allows them to be viable businesses. Oddly, the states don't allow their portals to collect success fees right now, clinging to an old rule that only broker-dealers can do that. This is, frankly, little more than a protection racket for the broker-dealer profession that needs to be broken up. Until that happens, state crowdfunding platforms—unlike their national counterparts—will be left with unworkable business models.

- Here's another no brainer: Legalize free speech. I'm serious. Securities law is filled with absurd limits on what companies can and cannot say to establish relationships with potential investors. These laws were conceived in an era when long-distance communication was mostly transacted by telegraphs and mail. The Internet has democratized the flow of information, and the time when little gnomes in securities departments can control that flow by issuing "permission slips" for sharing information, company by company, is over. Allow local companies and people to talk with one another about anything, any time. We're all adults now. Fraudulent claims and misrepresentations would still be prohibited and actionable. But if you're sharing truthful information about your business with potential investors, this is a wonderful relationship to be celebrated—not a problem to be squelched.

- Which brings me to another area for state policy: Education. States should provide grants to grassroots organizations that are prepared to teach residents how to become prudent, successful local investors. It's stunning how few businesses and people actually know about emerging local investment options. The many tools that states have used to discourage smoking or drunk driving—billboards, bus-stop signs, conferences, curricula, social media—should be deployed to encourage local investing. We all need to spread the word, and state support can speed things up.

Advocating for policy change may be more than you signed up for. I know, I know, you just want to put your money in your life. But there's a practical point here: The more you and others in your community can change the system—locally, statewide, and ultimately nationally—the better your returns will be. You can shape the system to make it easier for you to find, evaluate, and profit from local investments. Become your community's expert on local investing, engage in modest advocacy, and all kinds of new possibilities may open up.

And for the Finance Entrepreneurs . . .

I began the book by noting that the local investment revolution, while grounded in well-founded public distrust of Wall Street, also provides the most visionary leaders in the financial industry with tremendous new business opportunities. To expand the services of local banks and credit unions with DIY Accounts. To deploy new investment funds and stock exchanges in your states. To provide grassroots investors with better tools to evaluate local securities. To integrate local securities into mutual funds. To bundle local securities in new ways, including local futures and derivatives (hopefully with greater transparency than their predecessors). To design new ways of diversifying portfolios with interesting combinations of large and small companies.

The most creative among you might see ways of improving economies of scale in the local investment industry. You might put together a national fund of local funds. Or design one platform for local stock exchanges and replicate it in all fifty states. Or create a network of local banks that share

certain administrative functions, like a producer cooperative. Or launch a national consulting firm in the area of local
finance. Or open a business school that specializes in teach-
ing the skills required for cutting-edge financial institutions.

Some of your colleagues will dismiss local investing as a
carnival sideshow irrelevant to the real economy of global
businesses. That's great news! It means that you are likely to
come to this cutting-edge industry faster than your peers.
And by the time they realize their mistake, you will be com-
fortably and profitably building the next century's financial
system.

A Drugstore Success Story in Ohio

One book that is very helpful for beginners is *Self-Directed
IRAs: Building Retirement Wealth through Alternative
Investing* by Richard Desich, Sr. In the early 1980s, Desich
wanted to help his clients invest in local companies but
found that the fees being charged by other trust companies were astronomical. So, instead, he applied to the IRS
for permission to enable his own brokerage company to
serve as a custodian for Self-Directed IRAs. In 1984, he and
twenty-two other investors each chipped in $6,000 to pur-
chase a local drugstore in Lorain, Ohio, and each investor
made $200,000 over the following nineteen years—a return
that far exceeded that delivered by Wall Street. That success
motivated him to start providing the service to his clients,
and many other success stories have followed.

For the Rest of Us . . .

Here's a checklist I hope you will consider:

- *Commit* at least 1 percent of your life savings to local investment next year and to moving at least 1 percent more every year going forward.

- *Join* The Next Egg, where you will find hundreds of people like yourself asking and answering vexing questions about local investing. You also will find periodic commentaries from me on *www.MichaelHShuman.com*.

- *Recruit* a small group of friends, maybe five to ten, to join a group where you can share the many tasks needed for successful local investment. Together, you will collect ideas about local investment opportunities, evaluate them, commit funds, and compare notes on your progress. You might even consider converting your group into a formal investment club.

- *Introduce* your local, county, and state politicians to the action lists laid out earlier, and perhaps even give them a copy of this book (heck, my kids need the royalties for college). Better still, become a politician and make local investment reform your calling card.

- *Challenge* the financial experts in your community to figure out how they can join the local investment revolution and profit from it.

As you embark on this adventure, remember the immortal words of Sir Francis Bacon: "It would be an unsound fancy and self-contradictory to expect that things which have never yet been done can be done except by means which have never yet been tried."

NOTES

Foreword

1 Saadia Madsbjerg, "Why a Recession Would Be Good for ESG Investors," *Barron's*, June 21, 2019, *https://www.barrons.com/articles/recession-esg-investors-51561062809*.

2 Morgan Simon, "GEO Group Running Out of Banks as 100% of Known Banking Partners Say 'No' to the Private Prison Sector," *Forbes*, updated October 10–11, 2019, *https://www.forbes.com/sites/morgansimon/2019/09/30/geo-group-runs-out-of-banks-as-100-of-banking-partners-say-no-to-the-private-prison-sector/?fbclid=IwAR3ILh9D-MJum0w-o_JMgWNJhp1lELVHsYdRvWLdz38m7zZrfY6ZnVJ2OAo#600c82043298*.

3 Monica Tyler-Davies, "A New Fossil Free Milestone: $11 Trillion Has Been Committed to Divest from Fossil Fuels," 350.org, September 8, 2019, accessed November 25, 2019, *https://350.org/11-trillion-divested/*.

4 Ruth Pitchford, ed., "Pensions Funds Recouping Some of 2008 Losses," Reuters, October 26, 2009, *https://www.reuters.com/article/pensions-recovery-oecd/pensions-funds-recouping-some-of-2008-losses-idUSLNE59P00L20091026*.

5 Madsbjerg, "Recession Would Be Good," *https://www.barrons.com/articles/recession-esg-investors-51561062809*.

6 Emily Chasan, "Global Sustainable Investments Rise 34 Percent to $30.7 Trillion," *Bloomberg*, April 1, 2019, accessed November 25, 2019, *https://www.bloomberg.com/news/articles/2019-04-01/global-sustainable-investments-rise-34-percent-to-30-7-trillion*.

Introduction

1 Milton Friedman, "The Social Responsibility of Business Is to Increase Its Profits," *New York Times Magazine*, September 13, 1970.

2 Business Roundtable, "Business Roundtable Redefines the Purpose of a Corporation to Promote 'An Economy That Serves All Americans,'" press release, August 19, 2019, accessed September 26, 2019, *https://www.businessroundtable.org/business-roundtable-redefines -the-purpose-of-a-corporation-to-promote-an-economy-that -serves-all-americans*.

3 John Elkington, *Cannibals with Forks: The Triple Bottom Line of 21st Century Business* (Oxford: Capstone, 1997).

4 Georg Kell, "The Remarkable Rise of ESG," *Forbes*, July 11, 2018.

5 See, e.g., Ben Cohen and Jerry Greenfield, *Ben & Jerry's Double-Dip: How to Run a Values-Led Business and Make Money, Too* (New York: Simon & Schuster, 1998).

6 Fundera, a New York–based financial institution specializing in small business loans, claims that $17.2 billion is raised annually through crowdfunding sites in North America. See Maddie Shepherd, "Crowdfunding Statistics (2019): Market Size and Growth," Fundera, updated August 26, 2019, accessed October 4, 2019, *https://www.fundera.com/resources/crowdfunding-statistics*.

7 Crowdfund Capital Advisors, *The 2018 State of Regulation Crowdfunding: U.S. Securities-Based Crowdfunding under Title III of the JOBS Act*, January 24, 2019, accessed October 20, 2019, *https:// cdn.crowdfundinsider.com/wp-content/uploads/2019/02/CCA -2018-State-of-Regulation-Crowdfunding-Summary-FINAL.pdf*.

Chapter 1

1 This assumes single taxpayer rates for tax year 2018. For the higher tax bracket, the taxpayer pays $32,090 for his income up to $157,500 and 32 percent on the remainder. For the lower tax bracket, he pays $14,090 for his income up to $82,500 and 24 percent on the remainder.

Chapter 2

1 The total number of business establishments with employees in 2015 was 6,872,350, of which 1,251,702 had more than five hundred employees and were not considered small businesses. The total number of nonemployee businesses that year was 24,331,403. The 96 percent assumes that every business with more than five hundred employees is not locally owned. These data were calculated by combining the US Census Bureau's County Business Patterns (*https://www.census.gov/programs-surveys/cbp.html*) with its Nonemployer Statistics (*https://www.census.gov/programs-surveys /nonemployer-statistics.html*).

2 See note 1.

3 The most accessible free site providing access to the Dun & Bradstreet data, which also integrates several other national databases, is *www.youreconomy.org.*

4 Civic Economics, *Central Co-op: Feeding the Washington Economy II*, February 26, 2019, accessed September 27, 2019, *https:// www.centralcoop.coop/communityimpact/.*

5 The Institute for Local Self-Reliance nicely summarizes nearly a hundred relevant studies at *https://ilsr.org/key-studies-why-local -matters/* (accessed September 29, 2019).

6 Edward L. Glaeser and William R. Kerr, "The Secret to Job Growth: Think Small," *Harvard Business Review*, July–August 2010.

7 David A. Fleming and Stephan J. Goetz, "Does Local Firm Ownership Matter?" *Economic Development Quarterly* 25, no. 3 (2011).

8 Anil Rupasingha, *Locally Owned: Do Local Business Ownership and Size Matter for Local Economic Well-Being?* Community and Economic Development Discussion Paper, no. 01-13, Federal Reserve Bank of Atlanta, August 2013.

9 Mary Donegan, T. William Lester, and Nichola Lowe, "Striking a Balance: A National Assessment of Economic Development Incentives," Upjohn Institute Working Paper 18-291, 2018, 14.

10 Katie L. Halbesleben and Charles M. Tolbert II, "Small, Local, and Loyal: How Firm Attributes Affect Workers' Organizational Commitment," *Local Economy* 29, no. 8 (October 2014).

11 C. Wright Mills and Melville J. Ulmer, *Small Business and Civic Welfare*, Report of the Smaller War Plants Corporation to the Special Committee to Study Problems of American Small Business, U.S. Senate (Washington: U.S. Government Printing Office, 1946), quoted in Thomas A. Lyson, *Big Business and Community Welfare: Revisiting a Classic Study* (monograph, Ithaca, NY: Cornell University, 2001), 3.

12 Lyson, *Big Business and Community Welfare.* 14.

13 Thad Williamson, David Imbroscio, and Gar Alperovitz, *Making A Place for Community: Local Democracy in a Global Era* (New York: Routledge, 2003), 8.

14 Troy C. Blanchard, Charles Tolbert II, and Carson Mencken, "The Health and Wealth of US Counties: How the Small Business Environment Impacts Alternative Measures of Development," *Cambridge Journal of Regions, Economy and Society* 5, no. 1 (March 2012), 149–162.

15 J. Dara Bloom, Joanna Massey Lelekacs, Rebecca Dunning, and Emma Brinkmeyer, *Local Food Systems: Clarifying Current Research* (monograph, North Carolina State Extension, November 14, 2018).

16 Samuel Stroope, Aaron B. Franzen, Charles M. Tolbert II, and F. Carson Mencken, "College Graduates, Local Retailers, and Community Belonging in the United States, *Sociological Spectrum* 34, no. 2 (February 2014).

17 Richard Florida, *The Rise of the Creative Class* (New York: Basic Books, 2002).

18 Don Grant and Andrew W. Jones, "Are Subsidiaries More Prone to Pollute? New Evidence from the EPA's Toxics Release Inventory," *Social Science Quarterly* 84, no. 1 (March 2003), 162–73.

Chapter 3

1 "SOI Tax Stats: Integrated Business Data," IRS, accessed August 24, 2019, *https://www.irs.gov/statistics/soi-tax-stats-integrated-business-data*. The IRS does not report profits per se, but a rough

estimate is possible in all three business categories by dividing "Net Income (less deficit)" by "Total Business Receipts."

2 The most recent year available is 2009. Amelie Lafrance, "Firm Dynamics: Variation in Profitability across Canadian Firms of Different Sizes, 2000 to 2009," The Canadian Economy in Transition Research Paper no. 26, July 2012, Table 5, 7.

3 Board of Governors of the Federal Reserve System, *Financial Accounts of the United States, First Quarter 2019*, June 2019, 3. All the financial assets of US households and nonprofits now total about $85 trillion, and all their liabilities total $16 trillion. Banking assets include checking ($1.6 trillion), savings ($9.7 trillion), and money market funds ($1.8 trillion). Long-term assets include stocks ($15.6 trillion), bonds ($5.6 trillion), mutual funds ($7.9 trillion), pension funds ($25.7 trillion), and insurance funds ($1.7 trillion).

4 "Statistics at a Glance," Federal Deposit Insurance Corporation, accessed October 1, 2019, *https://www.fdic.gov/bank/statistical/stats/*.

5 Credit Union National Association, "U.S. Credit Union Profile," accessed October 1, 2019, *https://www.cuna.org/uploadedFiles /Global/About_Credit_Unions/NationalProfile-J19.pdf*; and Luis Dopico, *Credit Unions: Financial Sustainability and Scale* (Madison, WI: Filene Research Institute, 2016), accessed October 1, 2019, *https://www.researchgate.net/figure/Number-of-credit-unions -in-the-US-Actual-1910-2014-and-projected-2015-2025-annual _fig2_303687702*.

6 Stacy Mitchell, "Why Small Banks Make More Small Business Loans," Institute for Local Self-Reliance, February 10, 2010, accessed October 1, 2019, *https://ilsr.org/banks-and-small-business -lending/*.

Chapter 4

1 James Royal, "Best Investments for 2019," Bankrate, accessed August 24, 2019, *https://www.bankrate.com/investing/best-investments/*.

2 J.B. Maverick, "What Is the Average Annual Return for the S&P 500?," Investopedia, updated May 21, 2019, accessed August 24, 2019,

*https://www.investopedia.com/ask/answers/042415/what-average
-annual-return-sp-500.asp.*

3 Dave Ramsey, "Return on Investment; the 12% Reality," *Dave
Ramsey* (blog), accessed August 24, 2019, *https://www.daveramsey
.com/blog/the-12-reality.*

4 Ian Salisbury, "The Stock Market Hit Rock Bottom 10 Years
Ago. Here's How Much a $10,000 Investment Then Would
Be Worth Today," *Money Magazine,* March 8, 2019, accessed
August 24, 2019, *http://money.com/money/5637790/bull-market
-run-how-much-investment/.*

5 "Online Data Robert Shiller," Yale University Department of
Economics, accessed October 19, 2019, *http://www.econ.yale
.edu/~shiller/data.htm.*

6 Don't take my word for this: A spreadsheet with these data is available on my website, *www.MichaelHShuman.com.*

7 Mark Kolakowski, "The Stock Market Is About to Turn Ugly
for Investors: Shiller," Investopedia, updated June 25, 2019,
accessed September 8, 2019, *https://www.investopedia.com/news
/stock-market-about-turn-ugly-investors-shiller/.*

8 Between 1983 and 1990, in the US Investing Championships,
3,500 professional investors tried to outperform the S&P 500 for
a period of several months, and only a handful succeeded. In fact,
only 22 percent made any money at all! Ric Edelman, *The Truth
About Money* (Washington, DC: Georgetown University Press,
1996), 254.

9 More precisely, I mean a 5 percent return in a single year net
of fees and inflation. Since you will face taxes on all your gains
(except investing in your own home, which will reduce your taxes),
I do not assume that the 5 percent gain is net of taxes.

10 Board of Governors of the Federal Reserve System (US), "Commercial Bank Interest Rate on Credit Card Plans, Accounts
Accessed Interest [TERMCBCCINTNS]," retrieved from FRED,
Federal Reserve Bank of St. Louis, July 8, 2019, accessed September 8, 2019, *https://fred.stlouisfed.org/series/TERMCBCCINTNS.*

11 Lexington Law, "2019 Average Credit Card Debt Statistics in the U.S.," June 21, 2019, accessed September 8, 2019,

https://www.lexingtonlaw.com/blog/credit-cards/average-credit -card-debt-statistics.html.

12 Federal Reserve, "Federal Reserve Board Issues Report on the Economic Well-Being of U.S. Households," press release, May 22, 2018.

13 Zack Friedman, "Student Loan Debt Statistics in 2019: A $1.5 Trillion Crisis," *Forbes*, February 25, 2019, accessed September 8, 2019, *https://www.forbes.com/sites/zackfriedman/2019/02/25 /student-loan-debt-statistics-2019/#5ad5c387133f.*

14 Debt.com, "Student Loan Statistics," accessed November 24, 2019, *https://www.debt.com/student-loan-debt/average-statistics/.*

15 Robert J. Shiller, *Irrational Exuberance* (New York: Broadway Books, 2001), 22.

16 Steven Nadel, "For Existing Homes, Energy Efficiency Often Has a Better Return on Investment than Solar," American Council for an Energy-Efficient Economy, May 21, 2019, accessed September 9, 2019, *https://aceee.org/blog/2019/05/existing-homes-energy-efficiency.*

17 Diana Farrell and Jaana K. Remes, "How the World Should Invest in Energy Efficiency," *McKinsey Quarterly*, July 2008.

18 Christina Stowers, "Conserving Water, One Drop at a Time," Energy Saver, US Department of Energy, May 27, 2015, accessed October 4, 2019, *https://www.energy.gov/energysaver/articles/conserving -water-one-drop-time*; and "Fair Cost Guide: Low Flow Toilets," Homewyse, August 2019, accessed October 4, 2019, *https://www .homewyse.com/costs/cost_of_low_flow_toilets.html.*

19 "How Energy-Efficient Light Bulbs Compare with Traditional Incandescents," Energy Saver, US Department of Energy, accessed October 18, 2019, *https://www.energy.gov/energysaver /save-electricity-and-fuel/lighting-choices-save-you-money/how -energy-efficient-light.*

20 "Cost to Install a Thermostat," Homewyse, August 2019, accessed October 4, 2019, *https://www.homewyse.com/services/cost_to _install_thermostat.html*; and Allison Casey, "How Much Can You Really Save with Energy Efficient Improvements?," Energy Saver, US Department of Energy, October 7, 2016, accessed October 4, 2019, *https://www.energy.gov/energysaver/articles/how-much-can -you-really-save-energy-efficient-improvements.*

21   Aaron Kase, "How to Make Your Home More Energy Efficient with $1,000," Direct Energy, February 12, 2019, accessed October 4, 2019, *https://www.directenergy.com/blog/spend-1000-home-save -money-energy-efficient/*.

22   "How to Calculate Solar Panel Payback Period (ROI)," Energy-Sage, accessed October 3, 2019, *https://news.energysage.com /understanding-your-solar-panel-payback-period/*.

23   Michael Burge, "How Energy-Efficient Upgrades Can Increase Your Home's Value," NerdWallet, November 7, 2016, accessed October 3, 2019, *https://www.nerdwallet.com/blog/mortgages/6-energy-efficient -upgrades-increase-home-value/*.

24   Steven Deller, Ann Hoyt, Brent Hueth, and Reka Sundaram-Stukel, *Research on the Economic Impact of Cooperatives* (Madison: University of Wisconsin Center for Cooperatives, revised June 19, 2009).

25   Section 4(a)(2) of the Securities Act.

26   17 C.F.R. Section 230.251.

27   Section 3(a)(11) of the Securities Act.

28   This tax advantage, it's worth noting, effectively disappears if the bonds are held in a tax-deferred DIY Account. Some financial advisors suggest instead including *taxable* municipal bonds, which carry more risk and pay higher premiums.

29   Brian Beckon, Amy Cortese, Janice Shade, and Michael H. Shuman, *Community Investment Funds: A How-To Guide for Building Local Wealth, Equity, and Justice* (monograph, Pioneer Valley, MA: Solidago Foundation, January 2020).

30   Michael H. Shuman, *Open for Business: Building Local Economies through Place-Based Investing* (monograph, Oakland, CA: Confluence Philanthropy, 2016).

Chapter 5

1   A helpful calculator is available from Charles Schwab: *http://www .schwab.com/public/schwab/investing/retirement_and_planning /understanding_iras/ira_calculators/rmd* (accessed October 20, 2019).

2 Mat Sorensen, *The Self Directed IRA Handbook: An Authoritative Guide for Self Directed Retirement Plan Investors and Their Advisors* (Phoenix, AZ: SoKoh Publishing, 2014), 7.

3 There are currently more than fifty providers of Self-Directed IRAs. You can find lists of these providers at The Next Egg and on these three websites: *http://selfdirectedira.nuwireinvestor.com /list-of-self-directed-ira-custodians/*, *https://www.biggerpockets.com /rei/self-directed-ira-real-estate/*, and *https://www.innovativewealth .com/wealth-management/research/self-directed-ira-industry/the -ultimate-list-of-self-directed-ira-custodians-and-administrators/*.

4 Check The Next Egg for updates on this list.

5 Adam Bergman, *Going Solo: America's Best-Kept Retirement Secret for the Self-Employed* (self-pub., CreateSpace Independent Publishing Platform, 2019), 209–214.

Chapter 6

1 If you have full-time employees, The Next Egg can help you develop a retirement plan that offers DIY options to all your employees.

Chapter 7

1 A complete list can be found here: *https://www.finra.org/about /funding-portals-we-regulate* (accessed October 20, 2019).

2 Vermont Dollars, Vermont Sense (2015), which I cowrote with Gwen Hallsmith, is available for free here: *https://www.postcarbon .org/publications/vermont-dollars-vermont-sense/*. Washington Dollars, Washington Sense (2017), which I cowrote with Maury Forman of the Washington State Department of Commerce, is available for free here: *https://issuu.com/choosewa/docs/wadollarswasense-web*.

3 *First National Bank v. Estate of Thomas Philip*, 436 N.E. 2d 15 (1992).

4 *Swanson v. Commissioner*, 106 T.C. 76 (1996); *Hellweg v. Commissioner*, T.C.M. 2011-58 (2011). The shares in an LLC do not need to be new. The more recent case of *Ellis v. Commissioner* further established that it's acceptable if a Self-Directed IRA acquires a 98

percent share of the LLC while the other 2 percent is held by an unrelated person. T.C.M. 2013-245 (2013).

5 Department of Labor Advisory Opinion 1997-23A (1997).

6 *Repetto, et al. v. Commissioner,* T.C.M. 2012-1689 (US Tax Ct. 2012).

7 Department of Labor Advisory Opinion 2000-10A (2000).

Chapter 9

1 IRC Section 4975(e)(2).

2 Mat Sorensen, *The Self Directed IRA Handbook: An Authoritative Guide for Self Directed Retirement Plan Investors and Their Advisors* (Phoenix, AZ: SoKoh Publishing, 2014)

3 *Peek v. Commissioner,* 140 T.C. 12 (2013).

4 *Harris v. Commissioner,* T.C.M. 1994-22 (1994).

5 *In re Hughes,* 293 B.R. 528 (M.D. Fl. Bankruptcy Court 2003).

6 *Janpol v. CIR,* 101 T.C. 518 (1993); and *Peek & Fleck v. Commissioner,* 140 T.C. 12 (2013).

7 Sorensen, *The Self Directed IRA Handbook,* 47–49.

8 Sorensen, 33.

9 IRS Technical Advisory Memorandum 9208001.

10 *Lowen v. Tower Asset Management, Inc.,* 829 F.2d 1209 (2nd Cir. 1987).

11 DOL Advisory Opinion 2011-04A.

12 ERISA Advisory Opinion Letter 93-33A (1993).

13 Technical Advice Memorandum 9118001.

14 *Rollins v. Commissioner,* T.C.M. 2004-260 (2004).

15 See, e.g., *Etter v. J. Pease Construction Co.,* 963 F.2d 1005 (7th Cir. 1992*); Greenlee v. Commissioner,* T.C.M. 1996-378; and DOL Opinion Letter 88-018A.

16 IRC Section 4975(d)1.

17 IRC Section 1361(b)(1)(B), and IRS Letter Ruling 199929029, April 27, 1999.

18 IRC Section 408(m).

19 IRC Section 408(a)(3).

20 Sorensen, *The Self Directed IRA Handbook,* 97–109.

21 Internal Revenue Manual, Sections 4.72.11.1.2 and 4.72.11.1.3, Prohibited Transactions.

22 *Gregory v. Helvering*, 293 US 465 (1935).

23 CFR Section 2510.3-101.

Chapter 10

1 *Adams v. Commissioner*, 60 T.C.M. 996 (1973).

2 For example, the typical federal tax rate on C Corporations now is 21 percent of your taxable income (prior to the tax cut of 2017 it was 35 percent). Taxes on C Corporations generating under $100,000 of income annually can be significantly lower. So rather than create a small LLC and pay the UBIT, your Account might create a small C Corporation, pay a lower tax rate, and then distribute your income tax-free in the form of dividends. This is known, appropriately enough, as a "blocker corporation." Foreign corporations, facing lower national tax rates, also can be deployed for this purpose.

3 For example, you can find them here: *https://smartasset.com /retirement/how-to-calculate-rmd* (accessed October 18, 2019).

Chapter 11

1 Brian Beckon, Amy Cortese, Janice Shade, and Michael H. Shuman, *Community Investment Funds: A How-To Guide for Building Local Wealth, Equity, and Justice* (monograph, Pioneer Valley, MA: Solidago Foundation, January 2020).

RESOURCES

ORGANIZATIONS, BUSINESSES, AND WEBSITES PRO-MOTING LOCAL INVESTING

Cutting Edge Capital, *www.cuttingedgecapital.com*

Jenny Kassan Consulting & Coaching, *http://www.jennykassan.com/consulting-and-coaching/*

Investibule, *www.investibule.co*

Local Investing Resource Center, *https://www.local-investing.com/*

Locavesting, *www.locavesting.com*

National Coalition for Community Capital, *www.comcapcoalition.org*

The Next Egg, *www.thenextegg.org*

Revalue Investing, *www.revalueinvesting.com*

Slow Money, *www.slowmoney.org*

Sustainable Economies Law Center, *www.theselc.org*

BOOKS ON LOCAL INVESTING

David C. Barnett, *Invest Local: A Guide to Superior Investment Returns in Your Own Community* (self-pub., CreateSpace Independent Publishing Platform, 2014).

Amy Cortese, *Locavesting: The Revolution in Local Investing and How to Profit from It* (New York: Wiley, 2011).

Carol Peppe Hewitt, *Financing Our Foodshed: Growing Local Food with Slow Money* (Gabriola Island, BC: New Society, 2013).

Jenny Kassan, *Raise Capital on Your Own Terms: How to Fund Your Business without Selling Your Soul* (Oakland: Berrett-Koehler, 2017).

Michael H. Shuman, *Local Dollars, Local Sense: How to Shift Your Money from Wall Street to Main Street and Achieve Real Prosperity* (White River Junction, VT: Chelsea Green, 2012).

Morgan Simon, *Real Impact: The New Economics of Social Change* (New York: Bold Type Books, 2017).

Woody Tasch, *Inquiries into the Nature of Slow Money: Investing as if Food, Farms, and Fertility Mattered* (White River Junction, VT: Chelsea Green, 2008).

Elizabeth Ü, *Raising Dough: The Complete Guide to Financing a Socially Responsible Food Business* (White River Junction, VT: Chelsea Green, 2013).

BOOKS ON DIY ACCOUNTS

Adam Bergman, *Going Solo: America's Best-Kept Retirement Secret for the Self-Employed* (self-pub., CreateSpace Independent Publishing Platform, 2019).

Dyches Boddiford, Dorsie Boddiford Kuni, and John Hyre, The *Solo 401k: The Entrepreneur's Guide to a Powerful Pension Plan*, 4th ed. (Marietta, GA: Oaks Publishing, 2019).

William Bronchick, *How to Buy Real Estate (and Other Cool Stuff) in Your IRA* (Aurora, CO: Bronchick Consulting, 2014).

Richard Desich, Sr., *Self-Directed IRAs: Building Retirement Wealth through Alternative Investing* (Westlake, OH: Equity University, 2015).

Michael McDermott, *Live Tax Free Forever (through Your Solo 401k)* (self-pub., Party Island, 2010).

Mat Sorensen, *The Self Directed IRA Handbook: An Authoritative Guide for Self Directed Retirement Plan Investors and Their Advisors* (Phoenix, AZ: SoKoh Publishing, 2014).

ACKNOWLEDGMENTS

This book began almost a decade ago in Ft. Collins, Colorado, when I first met a financial advisor named Wes Dye. I had just begun to write *Local Dollars, Local Sense* and discovered that Wes, like me, was exploring new tools for helping clients invest locally. From that moment on, Wes began educating me about Self-Directed IRAs and Solo 401ks and pressing me to write a book on the topic. So thanks, first and foremost, to Wes for a decade of cheerful agitation.

I am grateful to the Lydia B. Stokes Foundation, particularly Nancy Deren and Tom Willets, for underwriting this work and for granting several generous extensions.

A big shout-out to our nonprofit sponsor, the Sun Valley Institute, particularly Aimee Christensen and her board, who made everything easy, giving me autonomy and support. You can—and should—read more about their projects on their website at *www.sunvalleyinstitute.org*.

I also appreciate the excellent research assistance I received from Audrey Dumentat and Jake Kornack. I benefited from sharp comments from various reviewers, including Amy Cortese, Audrey Dumentat, David Fisher, Travis

Higgins, Yonit Hoffman, Wendolyn Holland, Nathan Johnson, Mark Mowatt, Wendy Wasserman, and Jason Wiener.

If I got everything right, everyone named richly deserves credit. If I got anything wrong, you know where to find me.

INDEX

ABOUT THE AUTHOR

MICHAEL H. SHUMAN is an economist, attorney, author, and entrepreneur, and a leading visionary on community economics. He's director of local economy programs for Neighborhood Associates Corporation, a nonprofit affordable housing company, and currently an adjunct instructor at Bard Business School in New York City. He performs economic analyses for cities and businesses through Council Fire, where he's a senior associate. He is credited with being one of the architects of the 2012 JOBS Act and dozens of state laws overhauling securities regulation of crowdfunding.

He has authored, coauthored, or edited nine other books besides this one. One of his previous books, *The Small-Mart Revolution: How Local Businesses Are Beating the Global Competition* (Berrett-Koehler, 2006), received a bronze prize from the Independent Publishers Association for best business book of 2006. He also wrote a pioneering book on local investment called *Local Dollars, Local Sense: How to Shift Your Money from Wall Street to Main Street and Achieve Real Prosperity* (Chelsea Green, 2012).

A prolific speaker, Shuman has given an average of more than one invited talk per week, mostly to local governments and universities, for the past thirty years in nearly every US state and more than a dozen countries. He has appeared on numerous television and radio shows. Shuman has written nearly one hundred published articles for such periodicals as the *New York Times,* the *Washington Post,* the *Nation,* the *Weekly Standard, Foreign Policy, Parade,* and the *Chronicle on Philanthropy.* In 1980, he won first prize in the Bulletin of the Atomic Scientists' Rabinowitch Essay Competition on "How to Prevent Nuclear War."

Shuman received an AB with distinction in economics and international relations from Stanford University in 1979 and a JD from Stanford Law School in 1982. Between 1987 and 1990, he was a W. K. Kellogg National Leadership Fellow. He is also a member of the District of Columbia Bar.

ABOUT THE SPONSOR:
THE SUN VALLEY INSTITUTE

This book project is sponsored by the Sun Valley Institute, based in Sun Valley, Idaho. The Institute was launched in 2015 with a $250,000 grant from the Rockefeller Foundation and is led by Aimee Christensen, a former high-level director in the US Department of Energy. The Institute aims to be a center for public education, policy leadership, and investment to ensure economic prosperity, environmental protection, and human well-being in its home community of Idaho's Wood River Valley and beyond. The Institute is keenly interested in spreading best practices to increase community resilience in small towns across the United States and sees local investing (in such areas as food, energy, water resources, and manufacturing) as a critical tool.

Also by Michael H. Shuman

The Small-Mart Revolution
How Local Businesses Are Beating the Global Competition

Bigger isn't always better. Contrary to popular belief, small, locally owned businesses often outperform their "big box" and Fortune 500 competition—both in outright profitability and the value they bring to consumers, workers, and communities. Unlike mega-stores and multinational chains like Wal-Mart, these small businesses stimulate the economy by buying supplies and services locally, adapt to (rather than fight against) higher local environmental and labor regulations, and stick around for many years, often many generations. *The Small-Mart Revolution* details dozens of specific strategies small and home-based businesses are using to success-fully outcompete the world's largest companies.

Hardcover, ISBN 978-1-57675-386-6
Paperback, ISBN 978-1-57675-466-5
PDF ebook, ISBN 978-1-57675-542-6
ePub ebook, ISBN 978-1-60994-426-1

BK Berrett–Koehler Publishers, Inc.
www.bkconnection.com   **800.929.2929**

Berrett–Koehler
Publishers

Berrett-Koehler is an independent publisher dedicated to an ambitious mission: *Connecting people and ideas to create a world that works for all.*

Our publications span many formats, including print, digital, audio, and video. We also offer online resources, training, and gatherings. And we will continue expanding our products and services to advance our mission.

We believe that the solutions to the world's problems will come from all of us, working at all levels: in our society, in our organizations, and in our own lives. Our publications and resources offer pathways to creating a more just, equitable, and sustainable society. They help people make their organizations more humane, democratic, diverse, and effective (and we don't think there's any contradiction there). And they guide people in creating positive change in their own lives and aligning their personal practices with their aspirations for a better world.

And we strive to practice what we preach through what we call "The BK Way." At the core of this approach is *stewardship,* a deep sense of responsibility to administer the company for the benefit of all of our stakeholder groups, including authors, customers, employees, investors, service providers, sales partners, and the communities and environment around us. Everything we do is built around stewardship and our other core values of *quality, partnership, inclusion,* and *sustainability.*

This is why Berrett-Koehler is the first book publishing company to be both a B Corporation (a rigorous certification) and a benefit corporation (a for-profit legal status), which together require us to adhere to the highest standards for corporate, social, and environmental performance. And it is why we have instituted many pioneering practices (which you can learn about at www.bkconnection.com), including the Berrett-Koehler Constitution, the Bill of Rights and Responsibilities for BK Authors, and our unique Author Days.

We are grateful to our readers, authors, and other friends who are supporting our mission. We ask you to share with us examples of how BK publications and resources are making a difference in your lives, organizations, and communities at www.bkconnection.com/impact.

Dear reader,

Thank you for picking up this book and welcome to the worldwide BK community! You're joining a special group of people who have come together to create positive change in their lives, organizations, and communities.

What's BK all about?

Our mission is to connect people and ideas to create a world that works for all.

Why? Our communities, organizations, and lives get bogged down by old paradigms of self-interest, exclusion, hierarchy, and privilege. But we believe that can change. That's why we seek the leading experts on these challenges—and share their actionable ideas with you.

A welcome gift

To help you get started, we'd like to offer you a **free copy** of one of our bestselling ebooks:

www.bkconnection.com/welcome

When you claim your **free ebook**, you'll also be subscribed to our blog.

Our freshest insights

Access the best new tools and ideas for leaders at all levels on our blog at ideas.bkconnection.com.

Sincerely,

Your friends at Berrett-Koehler